Weeknight Cooking
with your Instant Pot®

Weeknight Cooking
with your Instant Pot®

Kristy Bernardo, founder of the *wicked* noodle

Simple, Family-Friendly Meals
Made Better in Half the Time

PAGE STREET
PUBLISHING CO.

PAGE STREET
PUBLISHING CO.

First published in 2018 by
Page Street Publishing Co.
27 Congress Street, Suite 105
Salem, MA 01970
www.pagestreetpublishing.com

Distributed by Macmillan, sales in Canada by The Canadian Manda Group.

23 22 21 20 19   5 6 7

ISBN-13: 978-1-62414-500-1
ISBN-10: 1-62414-500-0

Library of Congress Control Number: 2017914690

Cover and book design by Page Street Publishing Co.
Photography by Becky Winkler

Printed and bound in China

Instant Pot® is a registered trademark of Double Insight, Inc., which was not involved in the creation of this book.

For my Mom and Dad . . . for everything.

Table of Contents

Simple and Sophisticated Weeknight Sandwiches

Family-Friendly No-Meat Mains

Introduction

I'm often asked how I do what I do—how I can possibly create recipes, one after another, sometimes at the last minute. The question always makes me chuckle, and I explain that when you think about something twenty four hours a day, you make connections that you otherwise might not. A schoolteacher is always on the lookout for unique, interesting ways to engage students and will perhaps read something in a book or have an interaction with someone that sparks an idea. The same goes for food and creating recipes. A dish I enjoyed at a fine restaurant years ago could spark an idea today when I'm lost in thought at the meat counter. They say that you are what you think about, and I think a lot about food.

I grew up in central Wisconsin where meat, potatoes and a vegetable were always on the table for supper. We were free to roam about as we pleased, hopping on our bikes to ride the mile or so down to the river or explore the endless acres of forest and farmland that surrounded us. But make no mistake, we always had to be home once that dinner bell rang. Sharing a meal was what brought my family together, and that's still true today.

When I decided to write this book, it was my mom and dad who immediately came to mind. I knew they'd be incredibly proud of their small-town girl. Although I've lived all over the country, most notably having spent sixteen years in Southern California, I'll always be a Wisconsin girl. I've eaten at some of the finest restaurants in the world, and I've discovered the exquisite flavors of authentic tacos or barbecue at roadside stands around the United States. Yet my roots run deep, and that's where my true inspiration will always lie.

(continued)

Which brings me to the Instant Pot. When I first discovered it, I was amazed at the delicious food it could churn out in a fraction of the time. Practically anything you attempt to make with it—from hard-boiling eggs to chocolate pots de crème—magically becomes something delicious in minutes. It's a workhorse that will do almost anything you ask it to with ease! To quote my dad, who is surprisingly fascinated with it for someone who's never cooked anything in his life, "It's a fine piece of equipment."

The Instant Pot reminds me a little bit of, well . . . my own story. To look at it, you might think it's just another kitchen appliance. Yet it's able to produce dishes that can transport you anywhere and everywhere in no time at all. Thai, Mexican, Chinese or even a special dish from your childhood that you'd like to enjoy without too much effort. Those succulent ribs from your favorite barbecue joint can be easily re-created for a weeknight meal. A healthy soup that might otherwise take hours to simmer to get the flavors right, takes just twenty minutes! Similar to a small-town girl with deep roots who can travel the world, the Instant Pot is my solid, dependable sous chef who can create any number of dishes in no time at all. My Instant Pot has truly transformed the way I cook, and it will do the same for you.

These recipes were created for the busy, hectic weeknight schedules when you want to serve your family a delicious, home-cooked meal, but you don't have hours to prep and cook. It's meat, potatoes and vegetables—just like my mom used to make for our family. And I've added a few upscale twists that you'll be able to enjoy in a fraction of the time.

I hope this cookbook brings as much joy to you as it's brought me in writing it!

K Bernardo

You'd be hard-pressed to find someone who doesn't agree that meats cooked in an Instant Pot are quite remarkable. Chuck roasts that normally take hours to break down become tender in less than one hour under pressure. Ribs that are slow-cooked until the meat is falling from the bone take just thirty minutes! Even chicken breasts and pork chops, both notorious for being easy to dry out, turn tender and flavorful in no time at all.

Meat Lover's Mains

My 3 Favorites

Did you ever think you could use an Instant Pot for making ribs? I couldn't believe it the first time I tried them. I still love smoking ribs all day on my smoker, but nothing can top the feeling I get when I serve my family tender, fall-off-the-bone ribs in under an hour from start to finish.

30-Minute Fall-Off-the-Bone Ribs

COOK TIME
(UNDER PRESSURE)
30 minutes

YIELD
4 to 6 servings

½ cup (72 g) brown sugar, loosely packed

1 tbsp (15 g) coarse salt

3 tbsp (20 g) crushed black peppercorns

3 tbsp (20 g) smoked paprika

1 tsp cayenne

2 tsp (5 g) garlic powder

3 lb (1.4 kg) St. Louis–style pork ribs

1 cup (237 ml) apple juice

3–4 cups (709–946 ml) of your favorite barbecue sauce

1. Mix together the brown sugar, salt, pepper, smoked paprika, cayenne and garlic powder. Set aside.

2. With a paring knife, remove the membrane from the back-side of the ribs and discard. Cut the ribs into 2-rib sections. Generously cover the ribs with all of the rub.

3. Pour the apple juice into your pot, then place the trivet on top. Set the ribs on top of the trivet. Press "Manual" and adjust the timer to 30 minutes. Check that the cooking pressure is on "high" and that the release valve is set to "Sealing."

4. When the time is up, open the Instant Pot using "Quick Pressure Release." Brush the ribs with 1 to 2 cups (236 to 473 ml) of the sauce, then pop them under the broiler for about 5 minutes. Serve the ribs with the remaining sauce.

Pot roast was a typical meal I had growing up in rural Wisconsin. My mom would braise her roast all afternoon until the meat fell apart with just a fork. My version adds the twist of two of my favorite flavors: balsamic vinegar and Dijon mustard. The Instant Pot gets the pot roast as tender as my mom's in just 50 minutes! I've made this for her and she agrees that it's one of the best she's ever had. It also happens to be one of the most popular recipes on my blog, so be sure not to pass this one by.

Balsamic and Dijon Pot Roast

COOK TIME
(UNDER PRESSURE)
50 minutes

YIELD
12 servings

2–3 tbsp (30–45 ml) vegetable or canola oil

4 lb (1.8 kg) chuck roast

Kosher salt & freshly ground black pepper, to taste

1 large yellow onion, chopped

⅓ cup (80 ml) balsamic vinegar

2–3 tbsp (30–45 g) Dijon mustard

2 cups (472 ml) reduced-sodium beef broth

5 sprigs fresh thyme

1 lb (454 g) small baby potatoes, white or red (cut in half or quarters if golf ball–sized or larger)

2 bunches small carrots, with tops, about 1 lb (454 g) (cut off tops leaving a small stub)

1. Press "Saute" to preheat your Instant Pot and set to "More." When the word "hot" appears on the display, add enough vegetable oil to coat the bottom of the pot.

2. Season your chuck roast well with salt and pepper, add it to the Instant Pot and brown it well on all sides. If necessary to fit comfortably in the Instant Pot, cut your roast into 2 to 3 pieces and sear each piece separately. Remove the roast and set aside.

3. Reduce the heat setting to "Normal." Add the onions to the drippings in the pot and scrape up any brown bits on the bottom of the pot, adding a little more oil if necessary. Saute the onions until soft, about 3 to 5 minutes. Add the balsamic vinegar and boil it until it's reduced and slightly syrupy, about 2 to 3 minutes. Stir in the Dijon.

4. Set the roast on top of the onion. Pour in the beef broth and add the thyme sprigs.

5. Close and lock the lid of the Instant Pot. Press "Manual" and adjust the timer to 50 minutes. Check that the cooking pressure is on "high" and that the release valve is set to "Sealing."

6. When the time is up, open the Instant Pot using "Quick Pressure Release" and wait until all the pressure is released before opening. Working quickly, add the potatoes to the pot, followed by the carrots. Close and lock the lid of the Instant Pot. Press "Manual" and adjust the time to 10 minutes cooking time.

7. Season with salt and pepper to taste.

NOTE
This roast gets better with time so don't be afraid to make extra for leftovers!

If you love buffalo wings, you'll love this easy pasta dish. The Instant Pot makes it simple to enjoy those flavors without all the time and mess!

Buffalo Chicken Pasta

COOK TIME
(UNDER PRESSURE)
6 minutes

YIELD
6 to 8 servings

2 tsp (10 ml) extra-virgin olive oil

1 small onion, chopped

2 cloves garlic, minced

1 lb (454 g) penne pasta

4 cups (946 ml) chicken broth

4 cups (500 g) cooked, shredded chicken

8 oz (226 g) cream cheese, softened and cut into 8 pieces

1 (5-oz [150-ml]) bottle buffalo wing sauce (such as Frank's RedHot)

½ tsp coarse salt, or to taste

½ tsp freshly ground black pepper, or to taste

½ cup (61 g) crumbled blue cheese

2 tbsp (6 g) chopped fresh chives

1. Press "Saute" to preheat your Instant Pot. When the word "hot" appears on the display, add the olive oil, then add the onions. Cook, stirring occasionally, until the onions are soft, about 5 minutes. Add the garlic and cook about another minute, stirring frequently. Press "Cancel" to turn off the Instant Pot.

2. Add the pasta to the Instant Pot and pour the chicken broth over, taking care that all the pasta is submerged. Close and lock the lid. Press "Manual" and adjust the timer to 6 minutes. If you're using a different pasta, set the timer for half the time on the package cooking directions. Check that the cooking pressure is on "high" and that the release valve is set to "Sealing."

3. When the time is up, open the Instant Pot using "Quick Pressure Release." Stir the pasta, then add the chicken, cream cheese and wing sauce. Stir until completely incorporated and the cream cheese has melted and coated the pasta.

4. Season to taste with salt and pepper, then top with the blue cheese and chives.

Adding a little cream cheese to your pasta dishes will make them extra creamy. Sometimes I'll leave it out, or I'll add mushrooms or olives. This is an easy dish to make your own, so feel free to play around with it!

Cheesy Sausage Penne

COOK TIME
(UNDER PRESSURE)
6 minutes

YIELD
6 to 8 servings

1 lb (454 g) Italian sausage, casings removed

1 medium onion, chopped

1 red bell pepper, chopped

1 lb (454 g) penne pasta

4 cups (946 ml) chicken broth

4 oz (113 g) cream cheese, cut into 8 pieces

½ cup (90 g) shredded Parmesan cheese

1 (25-oz [709-g]) jar spaghetti sauce

½ tsp coarse salt

½ tsp freshly ground black pepper

½ cup (57 g) shredded mozzarella cheese

¼ cup (6 g) chopped fresh basil

1. Press "Saute" to preheat the cooker. When the word "hot" appears on the display, add the sausage, onions and bell pepper. Cook until it is lightly browned, about 5 minutes. Drain off any excess grease.

2. Add the pasta to the Instant Pot and pour the chicken broth over it, taking care that all the pasta is submerged. Close and lock the lid of the Instant Pot. Press "Manual" and adjust the timer to 6 minutes. If you're using a different pasta, set the timer for half the time on the package cooking directions. Check that the cooking pressure is on "high" and that the release valve is set to "Sealing."

3. When the time is up, open the Instant Pot using "Quick Pressure Release." Stir the pasta, then add the cream cheese, Parmesan, spaghetti sauce, salt and pepper. Stir until completely incorporated and the pasta is coated with sauce.

4. Finish your pasta one of two ways: Add the mozarella to the Instant Pot, put the lid back on and allow the cheese to melt, about 5 minutes. Alternatively, pour the pasta into a large baking dish, top with mozzarella and broil in the oven for a few minutes until the cheese is browned and bubbly. Top with the fresh basil.

This recipe is the reason my freezer always has at least one pack of chicken thighs in it. There's never a time when I don't have garlic, soy sauce and honey in my pantry, so having the meat on hand means I can make this any old time. I've even been known to use the Slow Cook setting on my Instant Pot first thing in the morning and leave it on low all day.

Honey-Garlic Chicken Thighs

COOK TIME
(UNDER PRESSURE)
6 minutes

YIELD
4 to 6 servings

2 lb (0.9 kg) skinless, boneless chicken thighs

⅓ cup (78 ml) soy sauce

⅓ cup (80 ml) honey

5 cloves garlic, minced

½–1 tsp crushed red pepper

Rice and vegetables, for serving

1. Cut off any excess fat from the chicken thighs.

2. Place the chicken in a single layer in the bottom of the Instant Pot. In a small bowl, whisk together the soy sauce, honey, garlic and crushed red pepper. Pour the sauce over the chicken, tossing the chicken to coat. Close the lid, press "Manual" and set the timer for 6 minutes, making sure that the Instant Pot is set to "high" and that the release valve is set to "Sealing."

3. When the time is up, open the Instant Pot using "Quick Pressure Release." Once the pressure is completely released, remove the lid. Remove the chicken and set aside on a plate tented with foil. Switch the Instant Pot to "Saute" and set it to "More." Gently boil until the sauce is thick, sticky and coats a spoon, about 7 to 8 minutes. Place the chicken back into the sauce and toss it gently to reheat.

4. Serve immediately over rice with a side of your favorite vegetables. I love steamed sugar snap peas with this.

SLOW COOK INSTRUCTIONS
Instead of pressing "Manual" on your Instant Pot, use the "Slow Cook" setting. Cook on "low" for 8 hours, then reduce the sauce until it's good and thick.

This flavorful, slightly spicy cabbage dish comes together in no time flat with your Instant Pot! This is a favorite of my dad's so I make it for him frequently. (Shhh . . . I'm giving my mom an Instant Pot for Christmas, so that she can make this for him all the time, too!)

Creole Sausage and Cabbage

COOK TIME
(UNDER PRESSURE)
2 minutes

YIELD
4 to 6 servings

2 tsp (10 ml) extra-virgin olive oil

1 (12-oz [40-g]) package precooked Andouille chicken sausage links, sliced

¼ cup (57 g) butter

1 small onion, chopped

1 clove garlic, minced

1 tsp creole seasoning

1 small green cabbage, chopped into large pieces

1 (14.5-oz [411-g]) can diced tomatoes

½ cup (118 ml) chicken broth

½ tsp coarse salt, or to taste

½ tsp freshly ground black pepper, or to taste

1 tbsp (4 g) chopped parsley.

1. Press "Saute" to preheat your Instant Pot. When the word "hot" appears on the display, add the olive oil, then the sausage; cook until it's lightly browned on both sides. Remove the sausage with a slotted spoon and set aside. Add the butter and onions; cook, stirring occasionally, until the onions are soft, about 5 minutes. Add the garlic and creole seasoning. Cook about another minute, stirring frequently. Press "Cancel" to turn off the Instant Pot.

2. Add the sausage, cabbage and tomatoes to the Instant Pot and pour the chicken broth over all. Close and lock the lid. Press "Manual" and adjust the timer to 2 minutes. Check that the cooking pressure is on "high" and that the release valve is set to "Sealing."

3. When the time is up, open the Instant Pot using "Quick Pressure Release." Season to taste with salt and pepper. You can drain off excess liquid if you prefer, but our family enjoys it so we leave it in. Garnish with chopped parsley.

This meatloaf has long been a family favorite and making it in my Instant Pot is a breeze! The combination of beef and Italian sausage gives great flavor, and I love that it has veggies baked right in. Make sure your veggies are cut into very small pieces to ensure they cook all the way through. It's perfect with Creamy Mashed Potatoes (page 126) and Two-Minute Maple-Glazed Carrots (page 135).

Loaded Veggie Meatloaf with a Balsamic Glaze

COOK TIME
(UNDER PRESSURE)
30 minutes

YIELD
6 to 8 servings

2 tsp (10 ml) extra-virgin olive oil

½ medium zucchini, diced

½ medium red onion, diced

½ yellow bell pepper, diced

½ red bell pepper, diced

2 medium carrots, diced

4 cloves garlic, minced

1 lb (454 g) ground beef

1 lb (454 g) ground Italian sausage

1 cup (108 g) panko breadcrumbs

2 eggs, beaten

¼ cup (10 g) chopped parsley

½ tsp kosher salt

½ cup (90 g) shaved Parmesan

¼ cup (61 g) ketchup

¼ cup (59 ml) balsamic vinegar

Creamy Mashed Potatoes (page 126) and Two-Minute Maple-Glazed Carrots (page 135), for serving

1. Press "Saute" to preheat the Instant Pot. When the word "hot" appears on the display, add the olive oil, then the zucchini, onions, bell peppers and carrots. Cook, stirring occasionally, until the vegetables start to soften, about 5 to 7 minutes. Add the garlic and cook about another minute, stirring frequently. Press "Cancel" to turn off the Instant Pot.

2. Place the veggie mixture into a large mixing bowl. Add the ground beef, Italian sausage, breadcrumbs, eggs, parsley, salt and Parmesan. Using your hands, mix until it's just incorporated. Form it gently into a meatloaf shape.

3. Place 1 cup (236 ml) of water in the bottom of the Instant Pot, then place the steam rack inside the pot. Fold two large pieces of tinfoil in half lengthwise, then overlap them in the middle to make a "plus" sign. Place the meatloaf in the center. Using the foil as handles, place the meatloaf into the Instant Pot on top of the steam rack, leaving the foil in place and folding it over as needed so as not to obstruct placement of the lid.

4. Mix together the ketchup and balsamic vinegar, then brush over the top and sides of the meatloaf.

5. Close and lock the lid. Press "Manual" and adjust the timer to 30 minutes. Check that the cooking pressure is on "high" and that the release valve is set to "Sealing."

6. When the time is up, open the Instant Pot using "Quick Pressure Release." Allow the meatloaf to rest about 5 minutes, then remove it from the pot using the foil handles. Slice it and serve with mashed potatoes and carrots.

This recipe is inspired by a local Greek restaurant we love. It has a deep, rich flavor that your family will love! It's so easy in your Instant Pot because you can do everything in one pot, from sautéing to cooking the chicken to reducing the sauce!

Mediterranean Chicken with Creamy Feta Sauce

COOK TIME
(UNDER PRESSURE)
6 minutes

YIELD
6 to 8 servings

2 tsp (10 ml) extra-virgin olive oil

¾ cup (120 g) chopped red onion

2 cloves garlic, minced

1 tsp dried basil

1 tsp dried oregano

1 tbsp (16 g) tomato paste

¼ cup (59 ml) white wine

2 cups (484 g) crushed tomatoes

¾ cup (177 ml) chicken broth

2 lb (0.9 kg) boneless, skinless chicken breasts, sliced crosswise into 1-inch (2.5-cm) pieces

2 cups (300 g) crumbled feta cheese

¼ cup (59 ml) heavy cream (optional)

2 tbsp (16 g) capers

¼ cup (45 g) chopped Kalamata olives

5 oz (141 g) fresh spinach leaves, about 4½ cups

Cooked orzo or rice, for serving

1. Press "Saute" to preheat your Instant Pot. When the word "hot" appears on the display, add the olive oil, then the onions. Cook, stirring occasionally, until the onions are soft, about 5 minutes. Add the garlic, basil and oregano. Cook about another minute, stirring frequently. Add the tomato paste and cook about another minute. Add the white wine and deglaze the pan, scraping any browned bits from the bottom of the pan. Cook another 1 to 2 minutes until most of the wine has evaporated. Press "Cancel" to turn off the Instant Pot.

2. Add the tomatoes and chicken broth to the pot and stir well. Nestle the chicken into the sauce.

3. Close and lock the lid. Press "Manual" and set the timer for 6 minutes, making sure that Instant Pot is set to "High Pressure" and that the release valve is set to "Sealing." When the time is up, open the Instant Pot using "Quick Pressure Release." Once the pressure is completely released, remove the lid.

4. Remove the chicken and set it aside. Press "Saute" and bring the sauce to a boil. Stir frequently and continue boiling until the sauce is thickened, about 5 minutes. Add the feta and stir until it dissolves into the sauce, then add the cream (if using). Stir in the capers, olives and spinach.

5. Add the chicken back to the pot. Serve the chicken over cooked orzo pasta or rice.

The first time I made this dish in my Instant Pot, I made it straight from my mom's handwritten recipe card. It's stained and brown from age, which makes this recipe even more special to me. When I made it for my mom in the Instant Pot, we both proclaimed it to be just as good as hers made the traditional way! And, trust me, that's saying a lot. I hope you enjoy this as much as my family and I do.

Mom's Chicken and Dumplings

COOK TIME
(UNDER PRESSURE)
10 minutes

YIELD
8 to 10 servings

3 lb (1.4 kg) chicken legs or thighs

4 carrots, chopped

4 celery stalks, chopped

1 medium onion, chopped

¼ cup (31 g) flour

2 tsp (10 g) salt

½ tsp pepper

4 cups (946 ml) chicken broth (the chicken should be almost covered, add more if necessary)

DUMPLINGS

1 cup (125 g) flour

2 tsp (7 g) baking powder

½ tsp salt

½ cup (118 ml) whole milk

2 tbsp (30 ml) vegetable oil

1. Press "Saute" to preheat your Instant Pot. When the word "hot" appears on the display, brown the chicken, in batches if necessary, about 3 to 4 minutes per side. Set the chicken aside. Add the carrots, celery and onions to the pot. Cook, stirring occasionally, until the onions are soft, 5 minutes or so. Add the flour, salt and pepper; cook about another minute, stirring frequently. Press "Cancel" to turn off the Instant Pot.

2. Add the chicken back to the pot and pour the broth over, taking care that all the chicken is submerged. Add a little more broth, if necessary. Close and lock the lid of the Instant Pot. Press "Manual" and adjust the timer to 10 minutes. Check that the cooking pressure is on "high" and that the release valve is set to "Sealing."

3. Meanwhile, make the dumplings. Mix together the flour, baking powder and salt in a medium-sized mixing bowl. Add the milk and oil, and stir just until incorporated. Be careful not to over-mix, which can make your dumplings tough.

4. When the time is up, allow the pressure to release naturally. Open the Instant Pot and gently stir. Switch to "Saute" mode, then drop in your dumplings by large spoonfuls, leaving them at the top. Don't stir them in. Put the lid back on for 10 minutes and simmer until the dumplings are cooked through.

Moroccan Chicken Thighs

COOK TIME
(UNDER PRESSURE)
10 minutes

YIELD
6 to 8 servings

3 lb (1.4 kg) skinless chicken thighs

1 tsp coarse salt

1 tsp freshly ground black pepper

1 small onion, chopped

2 cloves garlic, minced

1 tsp ground cinnamon

½ tsp ground ginger

1 cup (236 ml) chicken broth

½ cup (90 g) sliced green olives

½ cup (75 g) dried apricots

Zest and juice of 1 lemon

2 tbsp (8 g) chopped fresh parsley

3 cups (471 g) cooked couscous, for serving

1. Press "Saute" to preheat your Instant Pot. Season the chicken with salt and pepper. When the word "hot" appears on the display, brown the chicken on both sides in batches, about 3 to 4 minutes per side, then set the chicken aside. Add the onions and cook, stirring occasionally, until the onions are soft, about 5 minutes. Add the garlic, cinnamon and ginger. Cook about another minute, stirring frequently. Press "Cancel" to turn off the Instant Pot.

2. Add the chicken broth, green olives and apricots to the pot, then add the chicken. Close and lock the lid of the Instant Pot. Press "Manual" and adjust the timer to 10 minutes. Check that the cooking pressure is on "high" and that the release valve is set to "Sealing."

3. When the time is up, open the Instant Pot using "Quick Pressure Release." Remove the chicken from the pot and set it aside. Add the lemon zest and juice. Set your Instant Pot to "Saute" and boil the sauce, stirring frequently, until it's reduced and thickened, about 5 minutes. Stir in the parsley, add the chicken back to the pot and toss it to coat.

4. Serve the chicken over couscous and generously top with the sauce.

You will never cook pork chops another way once you make them in your Instant Pot! They come out very tender and eliminate dry pork chops forever. This makes a lot of sauce but, trust me, you'll love it so much that it will disappear. This recipe is delicious served with the Creamy Mashed Potatoes recipe in this book (page 126) as the sauce is amazing drizzled over the potatoes, too.

Pork Chops in a Dijon Pan Sauce

COOK TIME
(UNDER PRESSURE)
6 minutes

YIELD
4 servings

2 lb (0.9 kg) bone-in pork chops (3–4 chops; not too thick)

1 tsp coarse salt, or to taste

1 tsp freshly ground black pepper, or to taste

2 tsp (10 ml) extra-virgin olive oil

½ cup (118 ml) dry white wine

¼ cup (59 ml) low-sodium chicken broth

1 tbsp (15 g) Dijon mustard

½ cup (112 g) unsalted butter, cut into 8 pieces

¼ cup (10 g) chopped parsley

1. Season the chops with salt and pepper. Press "Sauté" to preheat your Instant Pot. When the word "hot" appears on the display, add the olive oil then brown the chops in batches on both sides, about 3 to 4 minutes per side. Remove the chops and set them aside.

2. Add the wine and stir to deglaze the pot, allowing the wine to reduce slightly, about 2 minutes. Add the chicken broth to the pot then return the chops to the pot, along with any accumulated juices.

3. Close and lock the lid of the Instant Pot. Press "Manual" and adjust the timer to 6 minutes. Check that the cooking pressure is on "high" and that the release valve is set to "Sealing."

4. When the time is up, allow the pot to release pressure naturally for 10 minutes, then release any remaining pressure using "Quick Pressure Release." Remove the chops and tent with foil to keep warm.

5. Press "Sauté" and allow the sauce to reduce by half, about 5 to 7 minutes. Stir in the Dijon. Add the butter two pieces at a time, stirring constantly until incorporated. Taste the sauce and season with salt and pepper, if necessary. Return the chops to the pot and toss them gently to coat with the sauce. Top with the parsley and serve.

You'll love cooking chicken thighs in your Instant Pot! They're not too thick so they cook quickly, plus they have a great flavor. This simple recipe is one of my girls' favorites.

Sesame Chicken

COOK TIME
(UNDER PRESSURE)
6 minutes

YIELD
4 to 6 servings

2 lb (0.9 kg) boneless skinless chicken thighs

¼ cup (59 ml) soy sauce

2 tbsp (30 ml) honey

3 tbsp (45 ml) mirin

3 cloves garlic, minced

1 tsp ground ginger

1 tsp sesame oil

2 tbsp (20 g) sesame seeds

2–3 green onions, sliced

Rice and vegetables, for serving

1. Remove any excess fat from the chicken thighs.

2. Place the chicken in a single layer in the bottom of the Instant Pot. In a small bowl, whisk together the soy sauce, honey, mirin, garlic, ginger and sesame oil. Pour the sauce over the chicken, tossing it to coat. Close the lid, and press "Manual." Set the timer for 6 minutes, making sure that the Instant Pot is set to "high" and that the release valve is set to "Sealing."

3. When the time is up, open the Instant Pot using "Quick Pressure Release." Once the pressure is completely released, remove the lid. Remove the chicken and set it aside on a plate tented with foil. Switch the Instant Pot to "Saute" and set it to "More." Gently boil until the sauce is thick, sticky and coats a spoon, about 7 to 8 minutes. Place the chicken back into the sauce and toss it gently to reheat.

4. Sprinkle the sesame seeds and green onions over the chicken. Serve it immediately over rice with a side of your favorite vegetables. I love steamed sugar snap peas with this.

Smoky-Spicy Rubbed Chicken

COOK TIME
(UNDER PRESSURE)
32 minutes

YIELD
6 to 8 servings

2 tsp (5 g) garlic powder

2 tsp (5 g) onion powder

2 tsp (5 g) ancho chile powder

2 tsp (5 g) smoked paprika

1 tsp cayenne pepper

½ tsp coarse salt

½ tsp freshly ground black pepper

2 tbsp (30 ml) vegetable or canola oil

4 lb (1.8 kg) chicken, cut up (any combination of breast, legs or thighs, skin on)

1 cup (236 ml) chicken broth

1. Mix together the garlic powder, onion powder, ancho chile powder, smoked paprika, cayenne pepper, salt and pepper in a small bowl. Stir in the oil to make a paste. Rub the paste underneath the skin of the chicken.

2. Press "Saute" to preheat your Instant Pot. When the word "hot" appears on the display, brown the chicken, in batches, about 3 to 4 minutes per side.

3. Pour the chicken broth into the bottom of the pot, scraping to release any brown bits from the bottom of the pot. Press "Manual" and adjust the timer to 32 minutes. Check that the cooking pressure is on "high" and that the release valve is set to "Sealing."

4. When the time is up, open the Instant Pot using "Quick Pressure Release." Remove the chicken and serve immediately.

This recipe is a riff on Swedish meatballs that's been streamlined for an easy, one-pot meal. The Instant Pot turns chuck roast into incredibly tender bites of beef for a delicious bowl of comfort food.

Swedish Beef and Rice

COOK TIME
(UNDER PRESSURE)
30 minutes

YIELD
6 to 8 servings

2 lb (0.9 kg) boneless chuck roast, cut into bite-sized pieces

1 tsp salt

1 tsp freshly ground black pepper

1 tbsp (15 ml) extra-virgin olive oil

1 medium onion, chopped

¼ tsp freshly grated nutmeg

¼ tsp ground allspice

¼ tsp ground ginger

¼ cup (30 g) all-purpose flour

4 cups (946 ml) beef broth

1½ cups (293 g) long-grain white rice

1 cup (230 g) sour cream

1–2 tbsp (4–8 g) chopped parsley, for garnish (optional)

1. Season the beef with salt and pepper. Press "Saute" to preheat your Instant Pot. When the word "hot" appears on the display, add the oil to the pot, then brown the beef in the pot in batches, about 6 to 7 minutes per batch. Remove the beef with a slotted spoon. Add the onions to the pot and cook, stirring occasionally, until the onions are soft, about 5 minutes. Add the nutmeg, allspice, ginger and flour. Cook for 2 minutes, stirring constantly. Slowly whisk in the beef broth. Add the browned beef and rice to the pot. Stir.

2. Close and lock the lid of the Instant Pot. Press "Manual" and adjust the timer to 30 minutes. Check that the cooking pressure is on "high" and that the release valve is set to "Sealing."

3. When the time is up, open the Instant Pot using "Quick Pressure Release." Stir the mixture and add the sour cream, stirring again to incorporate. Season to taste with more salt and pepper, and sprinkle chopped parsley on top, if desired.

Soups have always been one of my favorite things to make. I was pleasantly surprised by how simple they are in the Instant Pot! Most soups call for sautéing at least onions and sometimes a mirepoix as the base, and the Instant Pot's "Saute" function is perfect for this. And, because the Instant Pot automatically turns to the "Keep Warm" setting once the timer is up, you can make soup anytime and allow it to stay warm for up to ten hours, making it perfect for busy days or if you want soup ready when you get home.

Comforting One-Pot Soups and Stews

My 3 Favorites

With its bright lemon flavor and comfort-in-a-bowl creaminess, this delicious soup will be a family favorite. Avgolemono soup is a well-known Greek soup that you'll find on the menu in many Greek restaurants. It's easy to make in your Instant Pot so you can have it anytime! Use the black pepper liberally, if desired. The contrast with the lemon is wonderful.

Avgolemono (Chicken and Lemon Rice Soup)

COOK TIME (UNDER PRESSURE)
10 minutes

YIELD
8 to 10 servings

4 lb (1.8 kg) split, bone-in chicken breasts

2 carrots, cut into large pieces

1 leek, split and top discarded

1 medium onion, chopped

1 bay leaf

1½ cups (252 g) orzo pasta

⅓–½ cup (78–118 ml) fresh lemon juice, to taste

4 large eggs

2–3 tsp (10–15 g) coarse salt, or to taste

Freshly ground black pepper to taste

1. Place the chicken, carrots, leek, onion and bay leaf in your pot then fill with enough water to cover. Close and lock the lid of the Instant Pot. Press "Manual" and adjust the timer to 10 minutes. Check that the cooking pressure is on "high" and that the release valve is set to "Sealing."

2. When the time is up, open the Instant Pot using "Quick Pressure Release." Remove the chicken and set it aside to cool. Next, remove the carrots; enjoy them on their own or discard. Remove and discard the leek and bay leaf. Press "Sauté" on your Instant Pot and bring the remaining chicken stock to a boil. Add the pasta and cook 9 minutes or according to package directions.

3. Meanwhile, remove the chicken meat from the bone and discard the bones.

4. In a small bowl, beat the lemon juice and eggs together. VERY slowly, temper the eggs by whisking in 2 cups (472 ml) of the hot stock, taking care to whisk constantly so the eggs don't cook. Immediately pour the egg mixture into the pot and stir. Return the chicken to the pot, then generously season your soup with salt and pepper.

SLOW COOK INSTRUCTIONS
Instead of pressing "Manual" on your Instant Pot, use the "Slow Cook" setting. Cook on "low" for 8 hours or "high" for 4 hours, then continue with the remaining steps.

This chili is about as simple as you can get but it's loaded with flavor. The beef gets incredibly tender in the Instant Pot; your guests will think you simmered it on the stove all day! I like to serve it with a side of corn bread for dipping.

Beef and Poblano Chili

COOK TIME
(UNDER PRESSURE)
30 minutes

YIELD
8 to 10 servings

1 tbsp (15 ml) vegetable or canola oil

4 lb (1.8 kg) chuck roast, cut into bite-sized pieces

2 medium red onions, chopped

8–10 poblano peppers, stem and seeds removed, chopped

7–8 cloves garlic, minced

2 tbsp (16 g) chili powder

1 tbsp (8 g) ancho chile powder

1 tbsp (8 g) chipotle powder

2 tbsp (16 g) ground coriander

2 tbsp (16 g) ground cumin

2 tsp (5 g) smoked paprika

1 (24-oz [708-ml]) bottle Mexican beer (such as Pacífico)

4 (14.5-oz [411-g] each) cans fire-roasted diced tomatoes

Zest and juice from 1 lime

Salt and freshly ground black pepper to taste

1. Press "Saute" to preheat your Instant Pot. When the word "hot" appears on the display, add the oil, then brown the beef in batches, taking care not to crowd the pan. Cook about 5 minutes per batch. Remove the beef and set it aside. Add the onions and peppers to the pot. Cook, stirring occasionally, until the onions and peppers are starting to soften, about 5 minutes. Add the garlic, chili powder, ancho chile powder, chipotle powder, coriander, cumin and smoked paprika. Cook another 2 minutes, stirring frequently. Press "Cancel" to turn off the Instant Pot.

2. Add the beer, tomatoes, lime zest and lime juice to the pot. Close and lock the lid of the Instant Pot. Press "Manual" and adjust the timer to 30 minutes. Check that the cooking pressure is on "high" and that the release valve is set to "Sealing."

3. When the time is up, open the Instant Pot using "Quick Pressure Release." Season to taste with salt and pepper.

NOTE
For a thicker chili, simmer it on the "Saute" setting after the "Quick Pressure Release" until the chili reaches your desired consistency.

SLOW COOK INSTRUCTIONS
Instead of pressing "Manual" on your Instant Pot, use the "Slow Cook" setting. Cook on "low" for 8 hours or "high" for 4 hours, then continue with the remaining steps.

This easy soup is a delicious way to get more veggies in your diet. I wrote the recipe with plenty of cheese and cream—I am from Wisconsin, after all. You can scale them back if you prefer. Try roasting your broccoli before adding it to the pot, too.

Cheesy Broccoli Soup

COOK TIME
(UNDER PRESSURE)
20 minutes

YIELD
4 to 6 servings

1 tsp extra-virgin olive oil

1 medium onion, chopped

1 large head broccoli, cut into florets

1 medium russet potato, peeled and diced

1 (14.5-oz [411-g]) can chicken broth

2 cups (472 ml) heavy cream

2 cups (226 g) shredded cheddar cheese

1 tsp coarse salt, or to taste

1 tsp freshly ground black pepper, or to taste

1. Press "Saute" to preheat your Instant Pot. When the word "hot" appears on the display, add the olive oil, then the onions. Cook, stirring occasionally, until the onions are soft, about 5 minutes. Add the broccoli, potato and chicken broth to the pot.

2. Close and lock the lid of the Instant Pot. Press "Manual" and adjust the timer to 20 minutes. Check that the cooking pressure is on "high" and that the release valve is set to "Sealing."

3. When the time is up, open the Instant Pot using "Quick Pressure Release." Using an immersion blender, puree the soup until it's very smooth. Add the cream and shredded cheese; stir until the cheese is melted and the soup is smooth. Season well with salt and pepper.

NOTE
You can roast the broccoli before adding it to the pot for another layer of flavor. Toss your broccoli with just enough oil to coat, place on a sheet pan and roast it at 400°F (200°C, or gas mark 6) for about 20 minutes. I like mine a little charred for maximum flavor. Don't worry about overcooking it since it will be pureed in your Instant Pot later anyway!

SLOW COOK INSTRUCTIONS
Instead of pressing "Manual" on your Instant Pot, use the "Slow Cook" setting. Cook on "low" for 5 to 6 hours or "high" for 3 to 4 hours, then continue with the remaining steps.

This soup is filled with bright Southwestern flavors with the crunchy texture and sweetness of fresh corn. You'll be amazed that your chicken breasts will come out this tender in just 20 minutes of cooking!

Chicken, White Bean and Hatch Chile Soup

COOK TIME
(UNDER PRESSURE)
20 minutes

YIELD
6 to 8 servings

1 tbsp (15 ml) extra-virgin olive oil

1 medium onion, chopped

5 cloves garlic, minced

1 tsp ground coriander

2–3 lb (0.9–1.4 kg) boneless, skinless chicken breasts, cut crosswise into 1-inch (2.5-cm) strips

½ cup (85 g) chopped Hatch green chiles or canned green chiles

1 (16-oz [454-g]) jar salsa verde (such as Herdez brand)

3 ears of fresh corn, kernels removed and cobs discarded (about 2 cups [308 g])

1 (30-oz [848-g]) can white beans, rinsed and drained

2½ cups (590 ml) chicken broth

Juice of 1 lime

1 handful fresh cilantro, chopped

1 tsp coarse salt, or to taste

1 tsp freshly ground black pepper, or to taste

TOPPINGS (OPTIONAL)
Sliced avocado

Lime wedges

1. Press "Saute" to preheat your Instant Pot. When the word "hot" appears on the display, add the olive oil, then the onions. Cook, stirring occasionally, until the onions are soft, about 5 minutes. Add the garlic and coriander. Cook about another minute, stirring frequently. Press "Cancel" to turn off the Instant Pot.

2. Place the chicken on top of the onions, then add the chiles, salsa verde, corn kernels, beans, chicken broth and lime juice to the pot. Close and lock the lid of the Instant Pot. Press "Manual" and adjust the timer to 20 minutes. Check that the cooking pressure is on "high" and that the release valve is set to "Sealing."

3. When the time is up, open the Instant Pot using "Quick Pressure Release." Shred the chicken pieces with two forks. You can remove them from the pot to shred them if you like, but they're so tender that I don't find this necessary. Stir in the cilantro, then season well with salt and pepper. Serve with avocado and lime, if desired.

NOTE
Fresh corn will make all the difference in this soup, but feel free to use canned or frozen if that's all you have on hand.

SLOW COOK INSTRUCTIONS
Instead of pressing "Manual" on your Instant Pot, use the "Slow Cook" setting. Cook on "low" for 5 to 6 hours or "high" for 3 to 4 hours, then continue with the remaining steps.

Potato soup is on our dinner table often due to its ease of preparation, low cost and the fact that everyone in my family loves it. This recipe ups the flavor ante with chipotle, cheese and fresh corn. It's perfect for your Instant Pot because you don't have to bake the potatoes separately.

Chipotle Cheese Potato Soup with Fresh Summer Corn

COOK TIME
(UNDER PRESSURE)
15 minutes

YIELD
6 to 8 servings

½ lb (226 g) bacon, sliced into large pieces

½ medium-sized sweet onion, chopped

3 tbsp (23 g) flour

4 cups (946 ml) low-sodium chicken broth

3 lb (1.4 kg) red potatoes, quartered

2 ears fresh corn, kernels removed and cobs discarded

2 cups (472 ml) whole milk

1½ cups (170 g) shredded cheddar cheese

¼ cup (59 ml) adobo sauce from a can of chipotle peppers

1 tsp coarse salt, or to taste

1 tsp freshly ground black pepper, or to taste

TOPPINGS
Shredded cheddar cheese

Sour cream

Chopped green onion

Fresh chopped cilantro

1. Press "Saute" to preheat your Instant Pot. When the word "hot" appears on the display, cook the bacon until browned and crispy, about 8 minutes. Remove with a slotted spoon and set aside. Add the onions and cook until soft, about 5 minutes. Whisk in the flour and cook 1 minute.

2. Slowly whisk in the chicken broth, stirring to combine, then add the potatoes. Close and lock the lid of the Instant Pot. Press "Manual" and adjust the timer to 15 minutes. Check that the cooking pressure is on "high" and that the release valve is set to "Sealing."

3. When the time is up, open the Instant Pot using "Quick Pressure Release." Using a potato masher, mash the potatoes to thicken the soup to your desired consistency. Add the corn to the pot, then stir in the milk, cheese and adobo sauce until the cheese is melted and the soup is smooth. Season your soup generously with salt and pepper. Crumble the bacon over the top, then add desired toppings.

SLOW COOK INSTRUCTIONS
Instead of pressing "Manual" on your Instant Pot, use the "Slow Cook" setting. Cook on "low" for 5 to 6 hours or "high" for 3 to 4 hours, then continue with the remaining steps.

This soup will forever make me think of my mom. It's one of my lifelong favorites. I vividly recall watching her sauté the onions and add the flour; that was the moment I learned how to use flour to thicken a sauce. These days I raid her garden for freshly picked summer tomatoes which make this easy soup taste even more flavorful.

Creamy Fresh Tomato Soup

COOK TIME
(UNDER PRESSURE)
15 minutes

YIELD
4 to 6 servings

¼ cup (57 g) unsalted butter

1 medium onion, chopped

3 cloves garlic, minced

2 tbsp (15 g) flour

1 tbsp (14 g) tomato paste

2 cups (472 ml) chicken broth

5–6 large garden tomatoes

1 tsp sugar

½ cup (118 ml) heavy cream

1 tsp coarse salt, or to taste

1 tsp freshly ground black pepper, or to taste

¼ cup (56 g) prepared basil pesto

1. Press "Saute" to preheat your Instant Pot. When the word "hot" appears on the display, melt the butter, then add the onions. Cook, stirring occasionally, until the onions are soft, about 5 minutes. Add the garlic, flour and tomato paste and cook about another 2 minutes, stirring frequently. Press "Cancel" to turn off the Instant Pot.

2. Slowly whisk in the chicken broth, stirring to combine. Add the tomatoes and sugar. Close and lock the lid of the Instant Pot. Press "Manual" and adjust the timer to 15 minutes. Check that the cooking pressure is on "high" and that the release valve is set to "Sealing."

3. When the time is up, open the Instant Pot using "Quick Pressure Release." Using an immersion blender, puree the soup until very smooth. Stir in the cream, then season with salt and pepper.

4. Ladle into bowls and top with 1 to 2 teaspoons (5 to 9 g) basil pesto.

NOTE
Although I highly recommend using fresh tomatoes for this recipe, in a pinch you can substitute 3 (14.5-ounce [411-g] each) cans of fire-roasted diced tomatoes.

SLOW COOK INSTRUCTIONS
Instead of pressing "Manual" on your Instant Pot, use the "Slow Cook" setting. Cook on "low" for 5 to 6 hours or "high" for 3 to 4 hours, then continue with the remaining steps.

You may raise your eyebrows when you notice that there are a full two pounds (900 g) of mushrooms in this soup, but it's not a typo. They cook down significantly and their meaty texture will make it so you don't even miss the beef. The wine adds a wonderful depth of flavor despite the limited ingredients. Try adding some shaved Parmesan when you serve it; it looks so pretty and tastes delicious!

Mushroom Barley Soup

COOK TIME
(UNDER PRESSURE)
25 minutes

YIELD
8 to 10 servings

1 tbsp (15 ml) extra-virgin olive oil

1 lb (454 g) crimini mushrooms, thickly sliced

1 lb (454 g) white mushrooms, thickly sliced

1 medium onion, chopped

2 carrots, chopped

2 celery stalks, chopped

3 cloves garlic, minced

¼ cup (59 ml) red wine

1 (14.5-oz [411-g]) can fire-roasted diced tomatoes

¾ cup (150 g) pearled barley

6 cups (1.4 L) low-sodium beef broth

½ tsp coarse salt, or to taste

½ tsp freshly ground black pepper, or to taste

Shaved Parmesan, for topping (optional)

1. Press "Saute" to preheat your Instant Pot. When the word "hot" appears on the display, add the oil, then the mushrooms. Cook, stirring occasionally, until the mushrooms have released their liquid and it has evaporated. Add the onions, carrots and celery and cook, stirring occasionally, for 3 minutes. Stir in the garlic and cook another minute. Add the red wine and cook another 2 minutes. Press "Cancel" to turn off the Instant Pot.

2. Add the tomatoes, barley and beef broth to the pot, then close and lock the lid. Press "Manual" and adjust the timer to 25 minutes. Check that the cooking pressure is on "high" and that the release valve is set to "Sealing."

3. When the time is up, open the Instant Pot using "Quick Pressure Release." Season well with salt and pepper. Top with Parmesan, if using.

SLOW COOK INSTRUCTIONS

Instead of pressing "Manual" on your Instant Pot, use the "Slow Cook" setting. Cook on "low" for 7 to 8 hours or "high" for 4 to 5 hours, then continue with the remaining steps.

This is the only recipe in this book that uses fresh pasta instead of dried. I like to use fresh because I can stir it into the simmering soup just before serving, meaning I don't have to pay attention to my Instant Pot's beep if I have a busy night at home or step out for a little while. Sometimes I'll add some cooked sausage or cooked, shredded chicken at the end if I want a heartier meal.

Italian Tortellini Soup

COOK TIME
(UNDER PRESSURE)
15 minutes

YIELD
8 to 10 servings

1 tbsp (15 ml) extra-virgin olive oil

1 lb (454 g) sliced crimini mushrooms

1 large onion, chopped

1 carrot, chopped

1 celery rib, chopped

3 cloves garlic, minced

1 tbsp (14 g) tomato paste

2 (14.5-oz [411-g] each) cans fire-roasted diced tomatoes

6 cups (1.4 L) chicken broth

1 cup (236 ml) water

1 (9-oz [255-g]) package fresh cheese tortellini

2 cups (80 g) fresh baby spinach leaves

½ cup (90 g) grated Parmesan

1. Press "Saute" to preheat your Instant Pot. When the word "hot" appears on the display, add the oil, then the mushrooms. Cook, stirring occasionally, until the mushrooms have released their liquid and it has evaporated. Add the onions, carrots and celery; cook about 5 minutes or until the onions are soft. Add the garlic and tomato paste; stir well and cook 1 minute. Press "Cancel" to turn off the Instant Pot and remove the pot to a trivet to cool so the bottom doesn't scorch.

2. Add the tomatoes, chicken broth and water to the pot; stir well to combine. Return the pot to the base, then close and lock the lid of the Instant Pot. Press "Manual" and adjust the timer to 15 minutes. Check that the cooking pressure is on "high" and that the release valve is set to "Sealing."

3. When the time is up, open the Instant Pot using "Quick Pressure Release." Stir in the fresh tortellini and spinach. Allow the soup to sit for a couple of minutes, then serve with freshly grated Parmesan at the table.

SLOW COOK INSTRUCTIONS

Instead of pressing "Manual" on your Instant Pot, use the "Slow Cook" setting. Cook on "low" for 5 to 6 hours or "high" for 3 to 4 hours, then continue with the remaining steps.

Here's a soup you'll love to make when you want something with loads of healthy goodness but indulgent enough that you're treating yourself. The smoky sausage and salty Parmesan give a wonderful flavor twist. Add more pepper flakes if you like a little spice, and don't forget the extra Parmesan at the table.

Lentil Soup with Parmesan and Smoked Sausage

COOK TIME
(UNDER PRESSURE)
30 minutes

YIELD
12 servings

1 lb (454 g) smoked sausage, cut into bite-sized pieces

1 tbsp (15 ml) extra-virgin olive oil

1 sweet onion, chopped

4 carrots, peeled and chopped

2 celery stalks, chopped

2 tsp (3 g) dried basil

2 tsp (3 g) dried oregano

1 pinch of crushed red pepper flakes

4 cloves garlic, minced

2 cups (400 g) dried lentils

1 (28-oz [794-g]) can crushed tomatoes

6 cups (1.4 L) reduced-sodium chicken stock or broth

1 bay leaf

1 cup (180 g) freshly grated Parmesan, plus more for serving

Juice of ¼ lemon, or to taste

Kosher salt and freshly ground pepper to taste

Crusty bread, for serving

1. Press "Saute" to preheat your Instant Pot. When the word "hot" appears on the display, add the sausage and cook until it is lightly browned, about 5 minutes. Remove the sausage with a slotted spoon and set aside.

2. Add the olive oil, onions, carrots and celery to the drippings in pan. Cook, stirring occasionally, until the onions are soft, about 5 minutes. Sprinkle in the basil, oregano and red pepper flakes, and cook 1 minute. Add the garlic, and cook another minute.

3. Add the lentils, tomatoes, chicken stock and bay leaf, stirring well to combine. Close and lock the lid of the Instant Pot. Press "Manual" and adjust the timer to 30 minutes. Check that the cooking pressure is on "high" and that the release valve is set to "Sealing."

4. When the time is up, open the cooker using "Quick Pressure Release." Remove the bay leaf. Stir in the Parmesan and reserved sausage along with the lemon juice to brighten up the flavor. Season well with salt and pepper.

5. Serve with extra grated Parmesan on the side along with a loaf of crusty bread.

NOTE
Almost any sausage will work well in this soup. Try combining more than one sausage for endless flavor variations!

SLOW COOK INSTRUCTIONS
Instead of pressing "Manual" on your Instant Pot, use the "Slow Cook" setting. Cook on "low" for 7 to 8 hours or "high" for 4 to 5 hours, then continue with the remaining steps.

This soup is a perfect example of the kind of meal everyone loves to make on a cold winter's night. It cooks in just 25 minutes using the pressure cooking setting and turns out a thick, hearty soup to warm you up from the inside out. I'm a big fan of bacon, too, so I leave all the drippings in the pot for this one which adds a wonderful flavor.

Navy Bean Soup with Bacon

COOK TIME
(UNDER PRESSURE)
25 minutes

YIELD
12 servings

12 oz (341 g) bacon, sliced crosswise into ½-inch (1.3-cm) pieces

½ large sweet onion, chopped (or 1 whole medium)

2 carrots, sliced (halved first if large)

2 celery stalks, sliced (use and chop the leaves, too!)

3 cloves garlic, minced

1 (14.5-oz [411-g]) can fire-roasted diced tomatoes

1 (16-oz [453-g]) bag dried navy beans

8 cups (1.9 L) low-sodium chicken broth

1 bay leaf

Kosher salt & freshly ground black pepper to taste

1. Press "Saute" to preheat the cooker. When the word "hot" appears on the display, add the bacon and cook until it's crispy. Remove the bacon with a slotted spoon onto a plate lined with paper towels, then set it aside. Don't worry if you don't get every last piece of bacon; it's okay to leave some stragglers in the pot.

2. Add the onions, carrots and celery and cook about 5 minutes or so, stirring occasionally, until the onions are soft and translucent. Add the garlic, then stir and cook another minute. Stir in the tomatoes. Add the beans, chicken broth and bay leaf.

3. Close and lock the lid of the Instant Pot. Press "Manual" and adjust the timer to 25 minutes. Check that the cooking pressure is on "high" and that the release valve is set to "Sealing."

4. When the time is up, open the cooker using "Quick Pressure Release." Remove the bay leaf. Using an immersion blender, puree the soup until smooth. Alternatively, you can also use a food processor or blender and blend the soup in batches if necessary. Season the soup to taste with salt and pepper, and ladle into bowls. Top with the crispy bacon pieces.

SLOW COOK INSTRUCTIONS
Instead of pressing "Manual" on your Instant Pot, use the "Slow Cook" setting. Cook on "low" for 7 to 8 hours or "high" for 4 to 5 hours, then continue with the remaining steps.

Who wants the hassle of stuffing peppers? This easy soup is a deconstructed version of stuffed peppers that not only tastes just like them, I'm going to dare to say that it's even better! Plus, it's the perfect weeknight meal since it takes just 15 minutes of cooking time in your Instant Pot.

Stuffed Pepper Soup

COOK TIME
(UNDER PRESSURE)
15 minutes

YIELD
6 to 8 servings

1 lb (454 g) ground beef (grind your own, if possible)

2 bell peppers, chopped (any color)

1 small yellow onion, chopped

2 cloves garlic, minced

1 tsp dried basil

1 tsp dried oregano

1 tbsp (14 g) tomato paste

4 cups (946 ml) beef broth

2 cups (472 ml) tomato sauce

2 (14.5-oz [411-g] each) cans fire-roasted diced tomatoes

1 cup (210 g) uncooked white rice

Coarse salt and freshly ground black pepper to taste

1. Press "Saute" to preheat your Instant Pot. When the word "hot" appears on the display, add the ground beef, bell peppers and onions. Cook until the beef is browned and no pink remains. Add the garlic, basil, oregano and tomato paste and cook for 1 minute, stirring occasionally. Press "Cancel" to turn off the Instant Pot.

2. Whisk the beef broth into the pot and stir to scrape up anything sticking to the bottom of the pot. Add the tomato sauce, tomatoes and rice; stir well. Close and lock the lid of the Instant Pot. Press "Manual" and adjust the timer to 15 minutes. Check that the cooking pressure is on "high" and that the release valve is set to "Sealing."

3. When the time is up, open the Instant Pot using "Quick Pressure Release." Season generously with salt and pepper to taste.

SLOW COOK INSTRUCTIONS
Instead of pressing "Manual" on your Instant Pot, use the "Slow Cook" setting. Cook on "low" for 5 to 6 hours or "high" for 3 to 4 hours, then continue with the remaining steps.

Second only to my Instant Pot is my immersion blender for favorite kitchen appliance. I use mine constantly, mostly for delightfully smooth soups like this one. You can use a regular blender instead, but the ease of an immersion blender can't be beat. Don't skip the toppings for this creamy Thai soup; the peanuts add a wonderful texture and the flavors of the cilantro and lime bring it all together.

Thai Butternut Squash Soup

COOK TIME
(UNDER PRESSURE)
15 minutes

YIELD
4 to 6 servings

2 tsp (10 ml) extra-virgin olive oil

4 cups (560 g) chopped butternut squash

1 medium onion, chopped

3 cloves garlic, minced

1 tbsp (14 g) red curry paste

2 tsp (6 g) light brown sugar

½ tsp ground ginger

1 cup (236 ml) chicken broth

1 (13.5-oz [398-ml]) can coconut milk

2 tsp (10 ml) fish sauce

½ tsp coarse salt

½ tsp freshly ground black pepper

TOPPINGS

1 large handful cilantro, chopped

½ cup (80 g) chopped peanuts

Lime wedges

1. Press "Saute" to preheat your Instant Pot. When the word "hot" appears on the display, add the olive oil, then the squash and onions. Cook, stirring occasionally, until the onions are soft, about 5 minutes. Add the garlic, curry paste, brown sugar and ginger; cook about another minute, stirring very frequently. Press "Cancel" to turn off the Instant Pot.

2. Add the chicken broth, coconut milk and fish sauce; stir to combine. Close and lock the lid of the Instant Pot. Press "Manual" and adjust the timer to 15 minutes. Check that the cooking pressure is on "high" and that the release valve is set to "Sealing."

3. When the time is up, open the Instant Pot using "Quick Pressure Release." Using an immersion blender, puree the soup until very smooth. Season well to taste with salt and pepper.

4. Ladle the soup into bowls, and serve with the cilantro, peanuts and lime wedges.

SLOW COOK INSTRUCTIONS

Instead of pressing "Manual" on your Instant Pot, use the "Slow Cook" setting. Cook on "low" for 5 to 6 hours or "high" for 3 to 4 hours, then continue with the remaining steps.

I absolutely love making a big batch of flavorful meat for sandwiches. We usually do this once a week then use any leftovers for school or work lunches the next day. They work well for parties, too, since they can be left on the "Keep Warm" setting and guests can serve themselves. Be sure to use a good bread because that can make or break a sandwich!

Simple and Sophisticated Weeknight Sandwiches

Banh Mi is a Vietnamese sandwich and once you enjoy it, you'll be craving it often. Although it uses a short list of ingredients, the meat has an incredible flavor that you can eat as is, if you prefer. I like to use a pork rib roast for meat that's sliceable but still incredibly tender.

Banh Mi

COOK TIME
(UNDER PRESSURE)
50 minutes

YIELD
6 to 8 servings

3 lb (1.4 kg) boneless pork rib roast

1 tsp coarse salt

½ tsp freshly ground black pepper

½ cup (118 ml) chicken broth

½ cup (118 ml) soy sauce

1 tbsp (15 ml) fish sauce

¼ cup (36 g) light brown sugar, loosely packed

1 jalapeño, sliced

½ tsp ground ginger

6 cloves garlic, minced

FOR SERVING

Soft buns

Mayonnaise

Pickles

Cilantro

Sliced jalapeño

Sliced cucumber

1. Season the roast with salt and pepper. Press "Saute" to preheat your Instant Pot. When the word "hot" appears on the display, sear the pork roast on all sides, about 3 to 4 minutes per side. Remove the roast, set aside and press "Cancel" to turn off the Instant Pot.

2. Add the chicken broth, soy sauce, fish sauce, brown sugar, jalapeño, ginger and garlic to the pot, and stir. Nestle the roast back into the sauce, turning the roast to coat it with the sauce. Close and lock the lid of the Instant Pot. Press "Manual" and adjust the timer to 50 minutes. Check that the cooking pressure is on "high" and that the release valve is set to "Sealing."

3. When the time is up, allow the pressure to release naturally for 10 minutes, then release any remaining pressure using "Quick Pressure Release." Remove the roast and allow it to rest for 10 minutes, then slice it against the grain. Assemble the sandwiches and drizzle them with a little of the liquid from the pot.

What is it about tender beef topped with gooey cheese that is so perfect dipped in its own juices? The Instant Pot takes a fraction of the time to turn a tough roast into tender, flavorful meat for these sandwiches. This recipe makes quite a bit, but you can easily freeze the meat in individual portions to enjoy later . . . if you have any left!

French Dip Sandwiches

COOK TIME
(UNDER PRESSURE)
50 minutes

YIELD
8 servings

2 cups (472 ml) beef broth

3 lb (1.4 kg) chuck roast

1 tsp coarse salt

1 tsp freshly ground black pepper

2 large onions, thickly sliced

1 tsp garlic powder

½ tsp dried oregano

¼ tsp dried thyme

1 bay leaf

8 french rolls

8 slices provolone cheese

8 slices pepper Jack cheese (optional)

1. Pour the beef broth into your pot. Season the roast with salt and pepper, then set the roast in the pot, directly in the broth. Add the onions, garlic powder, oregano, thyme and the bay leaf.

2. Close and lock the lid of the Instant Pot. Press "Manual" and adjust the timer to 50 minutes. Check that the cooking pressure is on "high" and that the release valve is set to "Sealing."

3. When the time is up, allow the pressure to release naturally, then carefully open the pot. Slice or shred the meat, whichever you prefer. Pile the rolls with some of the meat then top with cheese, letting it sit a few minutes to melt the cheese, or pop it under the broiler. Serve the sandwiches with some of the liquid on the side for dipping.

The combination of toasted garlic bread, beef and blue cheese in this sandwich is over-the-top delicious. The balsamic onions bring it all together, but do plan ahead as you'll want to make them the night before. This roast beef also makes great deli sandwiches to take to school or work.

Garlic Bread Roast Beef Sandwiches with Blue Cheese and Balsamic Onions

COOK TIME
(UNDER PRESSURE)
50 minutes

YIELD
8 servings

1 tbsp (9 g) chopped garlic

1 tbsp (18 g) coarse kosher salt

1 tbsp (7 g) coarsely ground black pepper

¼ cup (62 g) Dijon mustard

3 lb (1.4 kg) boneless beef top loin roast, cut in half

1 cup (236 ml) water or beef broth

½ cup (114 g) unsalted butter, softened

1 tbsp (10 g) garlic powder

1 tbsp (2 g) dried parsley

8 ciabatta rolls, sliced

1 cup (122 g) crumbled blue cheese

2 cups (224 g) Balsamic Caramelized Onions (page 120)

Sliced fresh tomatoes (optional)

Arugula (optional)

1. Mix together the garlic, salt, pepper and Dijon. Using your hands, rub the mixture over the surface of the beef. Pour the water into your pot, then place the trivet on top. Place the beef on the trivet.

2. Close and lock the lid of the Instant Pot. Press "Manual" and adjust the timer to 50 minutes. Check that the cooking pressure is on "high" and that the release valve is set to "Sealing."

3. When the time is up, allow the pot to release pressure naturally for 10 minutes, then release any remaining pressure using "Quick Pressure Release." Remove the meat and slice it thinly.

4. In a small bowl, mix together the butter, garlic powder and parsley. Spread the mixture evenly over the cut sides of the rolls. Broil the rolls for a few minutes, cut-side up, until lightly browned.

5. Place a few slices of meat, some blue cheese and caramelized onions onto half the roll slices. Top with the tomatoes and arugula, if desired.

The first job I ever had was at The Wheel House back in my hometown of Waupaca, Wisconsin. They serve an incredible Italian beef sandwich that I still crave to this day. I don't get back to visit often enough, so when I can't take the craving anymore, I'll whip up this substitute. It's a very close second and I'm certain your family will enjoy it, too.

Italian Beef Sandwiches

COOK TIME
(UNDER PRESSURE)
60 minutes

YIELD
10 servings

4 lb (1.8 kg) boneless chuck roast

1 tsp coarse salt

1 tsp freshly ground black pepper

2 tsp (10 ml) extra-virgin olive oil

2 large sweet onions, sliced

3 cups (708 ml) beef broth

1 tbsp (8 g) Italian seasoning

2 tsp (5 g) garlic powder

1 bay leaf

1 (0.7-oz [19-g]) package dry Italian dressing mix

1 (16-oz [454-g]) jar pepperoncini peppers, with juice

TO SERVE
French rolls

Provolone cheese

1. Cut the roast into 4 pieces, then season it with salt and pepper. Press "Saute" to preheat your Instant Pot. When the word "hot" appears on the display, add the oil then sear the roast until browned on all sides, about 3 to 4 minutes per side, in batches if necessary. Press "Cancel" to turn off the Instant Pot.

2. Place the roast in the pot. Add the onions, beef broth, Italian seasoning, garlic powder, bay leaf and Italian dressing mix to the pot. Remove the stems from the peppers if desired, and add them to the pot.

3. Close and lock the lid of the Instant Pot. Press "Manual" and adjust the timer to 60 minutes. Check that the cooking pressure is on "high" and that the release valve is set to "Sealing."

4. When the time is up, allow the pressure to release naturally, then carefully open the pot. Shred the meat with two forks. Pile the rolls with some of the meat along with a few peppers from the pot. Top with a slice of cheese and let it sit a few minutes to melt, or pop it under the broiler. Serve with some of the liquid on the side for dipping.

This dish makes an exceptional sandwich but it's wonderful on its own, too. It's also delicious over rice or pasta. The Instant Pot makes it taste as if it's been simmering on the stove for hours after just 15 minutes of cooking time!

Italian Sausage and Pepper Sandwiches

COOK TIME
(UNDER PRESSURE)
15 minutes

YIELD
8 to 10 servings

2 tsp (10 ml) extra-virgin olive oil

2 lb (0.9 kg) Italian sausages

½ cup (118 ml) water

3 cloves garlic, minced

1 tbsp (8 g) Italian seasoning

2 cups (490 g) tomato sauce

2 (14.5-oz [411-g] each) cans fire-roasted diced tomatoes

2 red bell peppers, chopped

2 yellow bell peppers, chopped

½ cup (114 g) butter, softened

1 tbsp (10 g) garlic powder

1 tbsp (2 g) dried parsley

8–10 french rolls, halved

8–10 slices provolone cheese

1. Press "Saute" to preheat your Instant Pot. When the word "hot" appears on the display, add the oil, then brown the sausages, in batches if necessary, about 3 to 4 minutes per side. Remove the sausages and set them aside.

2. Deglaze the pot with ½ cup (118 ml) water. Add the garlic, Italian seasoning, tomato sauce and tomatoes to the pot; stir well. Add the sausages back to the pot.

3. Close and lock the lid of the Instant Pot. Press "Manual" and adjust the timer to 15 minutes. Check that the cooking pressure is on "high" and that the release valve is set to "Sealing."

4. When the time is up, open the Instant Pot using "Quick Pressure Release." Switch to "Saute" mode, then add the bell peppers and simmer about 5 to 10 minutes, or until the peppers are as tender as you like.

5. Meanwhile, mix the butter, garlic powder and parsley in a small bowl. Butter the cut side of the rolls, then broil them for a few minutes, cut-side up, until lightly browned.

6. Place a sausage and a generous amount of sauce onto a roll, then top with cheese and let sit a few minutes to allow the cheese to melt, or pop it under the broiler.

This recipe won me first prize in a recipe contest years ago. It's one that my friends and family are constantly telling me they made for their families or took to a party. It's a riff on buffalo wings, with the slaw replacing the blue cheese dressing and celery sticks. It's still one of my all-time favorite sandwiches—and so much simpler in my Instant Pot! Sometimes I'll double the recipe and freeze half for later.

Shredded Buffalo Chicken Sandwiches with Blue Cheese Celery Slaw

COOK TIME
(UNDER PRESSURE)
8 minutes

YIELD
4 to 6 servings

½ cup (114 g) unsalted butter

1 cup (236 ml) buffalo wing sauce (such as Frank's Red Hot), plus more for serving

2 lb (0.9 kg) boneless, skinless chicken breasts, sliced crosswise into 1-inch (2.5-cm) pieces

3 cups (672 g) coleslaw mix

1–2 celery stalks, diced

½ cup (61 g) blue cheese, crumbled

1 cup (220 g) mayonnaise

1 tbsp (15 ml) apple cider vinegar

1 tbsp (15 g) Dijon mustard

Coarse salt and freshly ground black pepper to taste

4–6 large buns

1. Press "Sauté" to preheat your Instant Pot. When the word "hot" appears on the display, add the butter and melt it completely. Stir in the buffalo wing sauce, then add the chicken breasts to the pot.

2. Close and lock the lid of the Instant Pot. Press "Manual" and adjust the timer to 8 minutes. Check that the cooking pressure is on "high" and that the release valve is set to "Sealing."

3. When the time is up, open the Instant Pot using "Quick Pressure Release." Shred the chicken with two forks and stir it to combine with the sauce.

4. Meanwhile, mix together the coleslaw mix, celery, blue cheese, mayonnaise, vinegar and Dijon. Season well with salt and pepper.

5. Top each bun with some of the buffalo chicken, adding more sauce if desired. Top with the blue cheese slaw.

Growing up in the Midwest, sloppy joes were a common sight on every dinner table. This is my slightly more grown-up version, using chipotle peppers for a smoky, spicy twist. Using an Instant Pot means you can set your timer for a short 10 minutes and walk away, instead of simmering and stirring for an hour or more.

Smoky Chipotle Joes

COOK TIME
(UNDER PRESSURE)
10 minutes

YIELD
6 to 8 servings

4 slices bacon

2 whole onions, diced

1 red bell pepper, diced

4 large cloves garlic, minced

3 lb (1.4 kg) ground turkey

3 tbsp (27 g) brown sugar

2 chipotle peppers, chopped

¼ cup (59 ml) adobo sauce from a can of chipotle peppers

1 (16-oz [454-g]) can tomato sauce

3 tbsp (44 ml) Worcestershire sauce

½ cup (118 ml) water

1 tsp kosher salt, or to taste

Freshly ground black pepper to taste

TO SERVE
Freshly baked buns

Sliced cheese

Jalapeño slices (optional)

1. Press "Saute" to preheat your Instant Pot. When the word "hot" appears on the display, add the bacon and cook until it's crispy, about 8 minutes. Remove the bacon with a slotted spoon and drain on a plate lined with a paper towel. Add the onions and bell pepper to the bacon grease in the skillet; cook until the onions are soft, about 5 minutes. Add the garlic and cook for 1 minute, stirring frequently. Add the turkey and cook until it is browned and cooked through.

2. Add the brown sugar, chipotle peppers, adobo sauce, tomato sauce, Worcestershire sauce, water, salt and pepper. Stir well.

3. Close and lock the lid of the Instant Pot. Press "Manual" and adjust the timer to 10 minutes. Check that the cooking pressure is on "high" and that the release valve is set to "Sealing."

4. When the time is up, open the Instant Pot using "Quick Pressure Release." Add the bacon, stir the sloppy joe mixture and allow your Instant Pot to stay on the "Keep Warm" setting. (Note: if it's not thick enough, simmer for 10 to 15 minutes on the "Saute" setting.)

5. Lightly butter the hamburger or slider buns and broil them, cut-side up, until lightly toasted. Top each bun bottom with some sloppy joe mixture, then top each with a slice of cheese and place under the broiler for 1 to 2 minutes until the cheese is melted. Add jalapeños, if desired.

These recipes are a great way to get more vegetables in your diet without skimping on flavor. My kids used to balk whenever I announced there wouldn't be chicken or beef on their dinner plates. Then I simply stopped mentioning it and they hardly noticed. Because these recipes are hearty enough to really fill you up, even the meat-lovers in your house will be happy!

Family-Friendly No-Meat Mains

My 3 Favorites

This is a recipe I've made for years and I make it even more so now that I cook with my Instant Pot. I made it for a kid's cooking class I used to teach, and it was always a hit with both the kids and their parents! I love the fact that it's a familiar comfort food but it also has that extra special something. It comes together so quickly in my Instant Pot, and I love that I don't need to sauté the squash separately anymore!

Butternut Squash Mac 'n Cheese

COOK TIME
(UNDER PRESSURE)
4 minutes

YIELD
4 to 6 servings

2 tsp (10 ml) extra-virgin olive oil

2 cups (280 g) diced butternut squash

1 small onion, chopped

1 lb (454 g) dried macaroni

4 cups (944 ml) water

1 cup (236 ml) whole milk

1 cup (236 ml) heavy cream

3 cups (340 g) shredded cheddar cheese (or more, see note)

1 tsp coarse salt, or to taste

1 tsp freshly ground black pepper, or to taste

1. Press "Saute" to preheat your Instant Pot. When the word "hot" appears on the display, add the olive oil, then the squash and onions. Cook, stirring occasionally, until the squash is soft, about 5 minutes. Add a couple of tablespoons of water if it starts to stick. Press "Cancel" to turn off the Instant Pot, then mash the squash with a potato masher until smooth.

2. Add the pasta to the Instant Pot and pour the water over, taking care that all the pasta is submerged. Close and lock the lid of the Instant Pot. Press "Manual" and adjust the timer to 4 minutes. If you're using a different pasta, set the timer for half the time on the package cooking directions. Check that the cooking pressure is on "high" and that the release valve is set to "Sealing."

3. When the time is up, open the Instant Pot using "Quick Pressure Release." Stir the pasta, then add the milk, cream and cheese; stir until completely incorporated and the cheese has melted and coated the pasta.

4. Season well with salt and pepper.

NOTE
If desired, you can transfer the mixture to a baking dish once it's done, top with a bit more cheese and broil for a few minutes until the cheese has browned.

This easy vegetarian dish is one I often make for myself on the rare occasion it's just me for dinner. In the summertime I'll raid my parents' garden and add a fresh chopped tomato, too. So much healthy goodness in one bowl, and it's done in just 7 minutes cooking time in the Instant Pot!

Pesto Parmesan Spaghetti Squash

COOK TIME
(UNDER PRESSURE)
7 minutes

YIELD
2 servings

1 cup (236 ml) water

1 medium-sized spaghetti squash, cut in half lengthwise and seeds removed

½ cup (113 g) prepared basil pesto

½ cup (90 g) shredded Parmesan cheese

Coarse salt and freshly ground black pepper to taste

¼ cup (34 g) toasted pine nuts (optional)

1 fresh tomato, chopped (optional)

1. Pour the water into the bottom of your Instant Pot, then place the steam trivet inside. Place the halved spaghetti squash on top of the trivet. I put one half in sideways to make them fit easily. Press "Manual" and adjust the timer to 7 minutes. Check that the cooking pressure is on "high" and that the release valve is set to "Sealing."

2. When the time is up, open the Instant Pot using "Quick Pressure Release." Using oven mitts, carefully lift the trivet out of the Instant Pot and set the squash aside to cool slightly.

3. Meanwhile, mix the pesto and Parmesan together in a medium-sized serving bowl.

4. When the squash is cool enough to handle, use a fork to pull the strands of squash. Place the squash strands in the bowl and toss with the pesto-and-Parmesan mixture. Season well with salt and pepper. Top with toasted pine nuts and fresh tomato, if you like!

This simple recipe is a light, summery dish that I often take to barbecues for my side dish contribution. The quinoa cooks in the Instant Pot in a short 2 minutes, making this a fresh, easy dinner or side dish. If you don't have goat cheese, feta is a wonderful substitute.

Bell Pepper and Asparagus Quinoa

COOK TIME
(UNDER PRESSURE)
2 minutes

YIELD
4 to 6 servings

2 tsp (10 ml) extra-virgin olive oil

1 small onion, chopped

2 red bell peppers, chopped

1 lb (454 g) fresh asparagus, tough ends trimmed and cut diagonally into ½-inch (1.3-cm) pieces

1 clove garlic, minced

1½ cups (255 g) quinoa

1½ cups (354 ml) chicken broth

½ cup (75 g) crumbled goat cheese

DRESSING

Zest and juice of 1 lemon

¼ cup (59 ml) high-quality extra-virgin olive oil

1 tsp coarse salt

½ tsp freshly ground black pepper

1. Press "Saute" to preheat your Instant Pot. When the word "hot" appears on the display, add the olive oil, then the onions, bell peppers and asparagus. Cook, stirring occasionally, until the onions are soft and the peppers and asparagus are crisp-tender, about 5 minutes. Add the garlic and cook another minute, stirring frequently. Place the pepper mixture into a medium bowl and set aside. Press "Cancel" to turn off the Instant Pot and rinse out the pot.

2. Press "Saute" to preheat the cleaned Instant Pot. When the word "hot" appears on the display, add the dry quinoa and "toast it," stirring frequently, about 5 minutes. Add the chicken broth and stir. Close and lock the lid of the Instant Pot. Press "Manual" and adjust the timer to 2 minutes. Check that the cooking pressure is on "high" and that the release valve is set to "Sealing." When the time is up, allow the pot to release pressure naturally.

3. Meanwhile, whisk the lemon zest and juice, olive oil, salt and pepper together. Open your Instant Pot and stir, then add the dressing and bell pepper mixture to the cooked quinoa. Season well with salt and pepper. Top with the goat cheese.

I love this dish because it works well as a weeknight meal or as a unique side dish for brunch or a pot luck. It's creamy with just a bit of smoky spice—my favorite combination. The slow-cook setting works best for this recipe, so usually I'll set the timer the night before and start it cooking on low so it's ready for us in the morning. It also makes a wonderful and different side dish for a Mexican dinner.

Chipotle Hash Brown Casserole

COOK TIME (SLOW COOK)
6–7 hours on low,
3–4 hours on high

YIELD
6 to 8 servings

2 tbsp (28 g) unsalted butter

1 medium onion, chopped

1 poblano pepper, chopped

1 lb (454 g) sliced mushrooms

2 cloves garlic, minced

4 oz (113 g) cream cheese, softened

2 chipotle peppers, minced

½ cup (115 g) sour cream

1 cup (236 ml) whole milk

1 tsp salt

½ tsp freshly ground black pepper

1 (20-oz [567-g]) package refrigerated shredded potatoes

1–2 cups (226–453 g) Mexican-blend shredded cheese

2 green onions, chopped

1. Press "Saute" to preheat your Instant Pot. When the word "hot" appears on the display, melt the butter, then add the onions, poblano pepper and mushrooms. Cook, stirring occasionally, until the mushrooms have released their liquid and it has evaporated. Add the garlic and cook another minute, stirring occasionally. Press "Cancel" to turn off the Instant Pot.

2. In a medium-sized bowl, mix the cream cheese, chipotle peppers, sour cream, milk, salt and pepper. Add the potatoes and stir to combine, then pour into the pot and mix well.

3. Close the lid of the Instant Pot. Press "Slow Cook" and adjust the settings to low for 6 to 7 hours or high for 3 to 4 hours.

4. About 30 minutes before the casserole is done, top it with the cheese. Continue cooking until the potatoes are soft and cooked through and the cheese is melted. Top with the green onions.

Risotto made in your Instant Pot turns out wonderfully creamy without all that stirring! This particular risotto is a wonderful springtime treat, especially if you can get your hands on fresh peas.

Creamy Lemon Risotto with Peas

COOK TIME
(UNDER PRESSURE)
6 minutes

YIELD
4 to 6 servings

1 tbsp (15 ml) extra-virgin olive oil

1 medium onion, chopped

2 cloves garlic, minced

12 oz (340 g) arborio rice

½ cup (118 ml) dry white wine

3 cups (709 ml) low-sodium chicken stock, room temperature

1 lemon (use the zest of the whole lemon and the juice from half)

2 tbsp (28 g) butter, cubed and softened

¼ cup (59 ml) heavy cream, room temperature

1 (9-oz [255-g]) package frozen peas (or the fresh equivalent)

Salt & plenty of freshly ground black pepper to taste

½ cup (90 g) shredded Parmesan

1. Press "Saute" to preheat your Instant Pot. When the word "hot" appears on the display, add the olive oil, then the onions. Cook until the onions are opaque and softened, about 5 minutes. Add the garlic and rice and cook about another 3 minutes, stirring frequently. Pour in the white wine to deglaze the pot and allow most of it to evaporate. Press "Cancel" to turn off the Instant Pot.

2. Pour the chicken stock into the Instant Pot, and close and lock the lid. Press "Manual" and adjust the timer to 6 minutes. Check that the cooking pressure is on "high" and that the release valve is set to "Sealing."

3. When the time is up, open the Instant Pot using "Quick Pressure Release." Stir in the butter, cream and peas, then season well to taste with salt and pepper. If you like pepper, go a little heavy here; it works well in this dish. Top with the Parmesan.

Alfredo Primavera

COOK TIME
(UNDER PRESSURE)
6 minutes

YIELD
6 to 8 servings

2 tsp (10 ml) olive oil

1 large onion, chopped

1 lb (454 g) sliced mushrooms

2 cloves garlic, minced

1 red bell pepper, chopped

2 carrots, diced

1 lb (454 g) penne pasta

6 cups (1.4 L) chicken broth

1 cup (236 ml) heavy cream

1½ cups (270 g) grated Parmesan

1 tsp coarse salt, or to taste

1 tsp freshly ground black pepper, or to taste

1. Press "Saute" to preheat your Instant Pot. When the word "hot" appears on the display, add the olive oil, then the onions and mushrooms. Cook, stirring occasionally, until the onions and mushrooms are soft, about 5 minutes. Add the garlic and cook about another minute, stirring frequently. Press "Cancel" to turn off the Instant Pot.

2. Add the bell pepper and carrots to the pot, then add the pasta and pour the chicken broth over, taking care that all the pasta is submerged. Close and lock the lid of the Instant Pot. Press "Manual" and adjust the timer to 6 minutes. If you're using different pasta, set the timer for half the time on the package cooking directions. Check that the cooking pressure is on "high" and that the release valve is set to "Sealing."

3. When the time is up, open the Instant Pot using "Quick Pressure Release." Stir the pasta, then drain in a colander to discard any remaining liquid.

4. Put the pot back in the Instant Pot unit and press "Saute." Add the cream, Parmesan, salt and pepper, stirring until the sauce is just starting to bubble and thicken. Put the pasta mixture back in the pot and stir until the sauce completely coats the pasta.

5. Season well to taste with more salt and pepper.

Pot pie has always been one of my favorite comfort foods. This version is easier than most as it takes just 15 minutes in your Instant Pot and uses packaged biscuits for the crust. Use frozen corn if fresh isn't available.

Fresh Veggie Pot Pie with Parmesan and Black Pepper Biscuits

COOK TIME
(UNDER PRESSURE)
15 minutes

YIELD
6 to 8 servings

1 tbsp (15 ml) olive oil

1 onion, chopped

1 lb (454 g) sliced mushrooms

3 carrots, chopped

2 celery stalks, sliced

2 cloves garlic, minced

8–10 red potatoes, cut into small, bite-sized pieces

3 cups (709 ml) chicken or vegetable broth

1 cup (236 ml) half & half

3 ears of fresh corn, kernels removed and cobs discarded (2 cups [308 g])

1 cup (227 g) green beans, trimmed and cut into small, bite-sized pieces

3 tbsp (28 g) cornstarch mixed with a few tablespoons of cold water (a slurry)

1 tbsp (15 ml) Worcestershire sauce

1 tbsp (15 ml) soy sauce

½ cup (90 g) grated Parmesan cheese

Coarse salt & freshly ground black pepper to taste

BISCUITS

1 (16.3-oz [462-g]) can refrigerated biscuits (about 8 large biscuits)

3 tbsp (42 g) butter, melted

2 tsp (5 g) freshly ground black pepper

½ cup (90 g) grated Parmesan cheese

1. Press "Saute" to preheat your Instant Pot and set to "Normal." When the word "hot" appears on the display, add the oil. Add the onions, mushrooms, carrots and celery. Cook, stirring occasionally, until the mushrooms release their liquid and it has evaporated. Add the garlic and cook about 1 minute, stirring frequently.

2. Add the potatoes and chicken broth to the pot. Close and lock the lid of the Instant Pot. Press "Manual" and adjust the timer to 15 minutes. Check that the cooking pressure is on "high" and that the release valve is set to "Sealing." When the time is up, open the Instant Pot using "Quick Pressure Release."

3. Switch to the "Saute" setting, then add the half & half, corn and green beans to the pot. Bring the mixture to a boil and add the cornstarch slurry. Don't add the cornstarch without first mixing it with cold water or it will be a clumpy mess. Stir constantly for about a minute or so to allow the sauce to thicken.

4. Stir in the Worcestershire sauce, soy sauce and Parmesan cheese. Season well to taste with salt and pepper.

5. To make the biscuits, place them on a large sheet pan at least an inch (2.5 cm) apart. Baste the biscuits liberally with butter, then sprinkle the tops with freshly ground black pepper. Spoon about a tablespoon (5 g) of Parmesan cheese onto each biscuit and spread it with the back of the spoon to cover the top. Bake them according to the directions on the package. Top each bowl of pot pie filling with a pepper-Parmesan biscuit.

This simple pasta salad is perfect for weeknight dinners because you can make it all in your Instant Pot, without the need for a separate skillet for sautéing. It can be enjoyed hot, cold or at room temperature, so you won't have to time it perfectly if everyone is arriving home at different times. It's also a great choice for a potluck or a holiday party.

Sun-Dried Tomato Orzo Pasta

COOK TIME
(UNDER PRESSURE)
6 minutes

YIELD
4 to 6 servings

2 tsp (10 ml) extra-virgin olive oil

1 onion, chopped

2 cloves garlic, minced

1 tbsp (5 g) oregano

½ cup (119 ml) white wine

1 (14.5-oz [411-g]) can fire-roasted diced tomatoes

½ cup (55 g) sun-dried tomatoes, chopped

1 cup (236 ml) chicken or vegetable broth

1½ cups (252 g) dried orzo pasta

Zest and juice of 1 lemon

½ cup (90 g) sliced Kalamata olives

½ cup (75 g) crumbled feta cheese

½ tsp coarse salt, or to taste

½ tsp freshly ground black pepper, or to taste

1. Press "Saute" to preheat your Instant Pot. When the word "hot" appears on the display, add the olive oil, then the onions. Cook, stirring occasionally, until the onions are soft, about 5 minutes. Add the garlic and oregano. Cook about another minute, stirring frequently. Press "Cancel" to turn off the Instant Pot.

2. Immediately add the wine to the Instant Pot to deglaze the pot; the pot will still be hot even though you've turned it off. Add the tomatoes, sun-dried tomatoes, chicken broth and orzo pasta to the pot and gently stir. Close and lock the lid of the Instant Pot. Press "Manual" and adjust the timer to 6 minutes. Check that the cooking pressure is on "high" and that the release valve is set to "Sealing."

3. When the time is up, open the Instant Pot using "Quick Pressure Release." Stir the pasta, then add the lemon zest, lemon juice, olives and feta.

4. Season well with salt and pepper.

Although this lasagna is intentionally all veggies, feel free to brown some Italian sausage with the onions if you're a meat lover. I guarantee that once you make lasagna in your Instant Pot, you'll never have it any other way! It cooks in just 20 minutes and the size is perfect for a family of four. If you own more than one Instant Pot, consider making two at once and freezing one.

Vegetable Lasagna

COOK TIME (UNDER PRESSURE)
20 minutes

YIELD
4 to 6 servings

2 tsp (10 ml) extra-virgin olive oil

1 small onion, chopped

2 cloves garlic, minced

2 cups (272 ml) spaghetti sauce

½ tsp coarse salt

½ tsp freshly ground black pepper

1 cup (123 g) ricotta cheese

1 large egg

1 cup (180 g) grated Parmesan cheese

1 medium zucchini, chopped small

1 medium yellow squash, chopped small

1 cup (149 g) roasted red peppers, chopped

8 oz (226 g) no-boil lasagna noodles

1 cup (133 g) shredded mozzarella

1. Press "Saute" to preheat your Instant Pot. When the word "hot" appears on the display, add the olive oil, then the onions. Cook, stirring occasionally, until the onions are soft, about 5 minutes. Add the garlic and cook about another minute, stirring frequently. Press "Cancel" to turn off the Instant Pot.

2. Place the onion mixture into a medium-sized mixing bowl. Stir in the spaghetti sauce, salt and pepper. In another small bowl, mix together the ricotta cheese, egg and Parmesan until smooth.

3. Grease a round 7-inch (18-cm) baking pan. Place a thin layer of the sauce onto the bottom of the pan. Top with one layer each of lasagna noodles, then the ricotta mixture, followed by a layer of vegetables (the zucchini, squash and roasted red peppers). Continue layering twice more, ending with the sauce, and pressing down gently each time you add a layer of lasagna noodles. Top with the shredded mozzarella.

4. Pour 1 cup (236 ml) of water into the bottom of the Instant Pot, then place the trivet inside. Make a foil sling out of tinfoil—a long piece of tinfoil folded twice lengthwise. Place the baking pan on top. Cover the baking pan with additional foil, then, using the sling, carefully set the pan onto the trivet, folding down any tinfoil so that it doesn't interfere with closing the lid.

5. Close the lid, press "Manual" and adjust the timer to 20 minutes. Check that the cooking pressure is on "high" and that the release valve is set to "Sealing."

6. When the time is up, allow the Instant Pot to naturally release pressure for 10 minutes, then open the Instant Pot using "Quick Pressure Release." Using the foil sling as handles, carefully remove the lasagna from the Instant Pot. Remove the foil, and pop the lasagna under the broiler a few minutes to brown the cheese. Allow the lasagna to rest for 10 minutes before serving.

If I had to choose one cuisine to both cook and eat for the rest of my life, it would be Mexican. I find the flavor profiles easiest to work with, and it's so simple to turn out amazing dishes that everyone will love. I'll adjust the spice levels for a crowd, or I'll keep it spicy if it's just for my family. Have a taco night with family and let everyone load up their own toppings! I promise it'll be a fun fiesta! I've especially always loved braising meats for tacos and other Mexican dishes, and using the Instant Pot means that you can make these time-consuming dishes even on a busy weeknight!

Quick and Delicious Mexican Meals

My 3 Favorites

We used to drive down to Rosarito, Mexico, at least once a month when I lived in Southern California just to get these tacos. They're simple without any fuss, just the way they serve them there. Add an ice cold Pacífico or Corona with a lime and it's the perfect Mexican treat. The recipe makes plenty of steak for filling tacos, so you can plan to have tacos another night or even use the leftover meat to serve with eggs for breakfast.

Carne Asada Tacos

COOK TIME
(UNDER PRESSURE)
20 minutes

YIELD
8 to 10 servings

STEAK

3 lb (1.4 kg) flank steak, cut into 2 or 3 large pieces

Coarse salt to taste

Freshly ground black pepper to taste

Juice from 3 limes

1 cup (226 ml) beef broth

TOMATILLO SAUCE

1 lb (454 g) fresh tomatillos, husked, rinsed and halved

1 jalapeño

1 clove garlic

2 tbsp (30 ml) extra-virgin olive oil

½ cup (7 g) fresh cilantro

1 tsp coarse salt

1 tsp freshly ground black pepper

FOR SERVING

Corn tortillas

Chopped white onion

Chopped cilantro

Sliced avocado

1. Place the steak in a large baking dish and season both sides with coarse salt and freshly ground black pepper. Squeeze the lime juice over the steak and refrigerate for 30 minutes.

2. Meanwhile, make the tomatillo sauce. Preheat the oven to broil and place the tomatillos cut-side down on a sheet pan. Add the jalapeño and garlic and drizzle with the olive oil. Broil for 5 to 7 minutes, or until charred and blackened in spots. Place in a high-powered blender along with the cilantro, salt and pepper. Puree until very smooth.

3. Put the steak in the Instant Pot and pour in the beef broth. Close and lock the lid. Press "Manual" and adjust the timer to 20 minutes. Check that the cooking pressure is on "high" and that the release valve is set to "Sealing."

4. When the time is up, allow the Instant Pot to naturally release pressure for 10 minutes, then release any remaining pressure. Carefully open the lid and remove the steak. The liquid can be discarded. Allow the steak to rest for 10 minutes, then thinly slice it against the grain.

5. Grill the tortillas, if desired. Assemble the tacos by putting a few slices of steak and some onion, cilantro and avocado in a corn tortilla. Top with the tomatillo mixture.

I fell in love with carnitas when I lived in Southern California. The subtle citrus flavor is to die for! Ever since I began cooking with my Instant Pot, I make this often because it's so simple and takes just a fraction of the time.

Carnitas Tacos with Quick Pickled Onions

COOK TIME
(UNDER PRESSURE)
60 minutes

YIELD
8 to 10 servings

PICKLED ONIONS

½ cup (118 ml) cider vinegar

1 tbsp (12 g) sugar

1 tsp coarse salt

1 medium red onion, sliced

CARNITAS TACOS

4 lb (1.8 kg) boneless pork shoulder

1 medium white onion, chopped

3 cloves garlic, minced

1 jalapeño, sliced

1 tbsp (5 g) Mexican oregano

1 tsp cumin

1 (12-oz [177-ml]) bottle Mexican beer (such as Pacífico)

Zest and juice of 1 large navel orange

Zest and juice of 1 lime

FOR SERVING

Corn tortillas

Queso fresco

Salsa verde

Chopped cilantro

Sliced jalapeños

1. In a small bowl, mix together the vinegar, sugar and salt. Add the onions and soak them at room temperature for at least 1 hour.

2. Cut the pork shoulder into 8 pieces, then place it in the bottom of your Instant Pot. Top with the onions, garlic, jalapeño, oregano and cumin. Pour the beer over all, then add the zest and juice of the orange and lime.

3. Close and lock the lid of the Instant Pot. Press "Manual" and adjust the timer to 60 minutes. Check that the cooking pressure is on "high" and that the release valve is set to "Sealing."

4. When the time is up, open the Instant Pot using "Quick Pressure Release." Remove the pork from the pot and shred it. Place the pork on a large sheet pan and drizzle with a small amount of the liquid from the pot. Broil the pork about 3 to 4 inches (7.5 to 10 cm) from the heat source, until starting to crisp slightly, about 5 to 7 minutes. Stir the pork, then broil again until starting to crisp. Stir the pork one more time, broil again until starting to crisp on top, adding a small amount of liquid if it looks too dry.

5. Place the carnitas in corn tortillas and top them with pickled onions, queso fresco, salsa verde, cilantro and jalapeños.

*See photo on page 98.

The simple flavors of traditional pot pie make it a great candidate for a Mexican twist. It's not spicy, so it's still a great family dinner choice.

Mexican Pot Pie

COOK TIME
(UNDER PRESSURE)
15 minutes

YIELD
6 to 8 servings

1 tbsp (15 ml) olive oil

1 onion, chopped

2 poblano peppers, chopped

1 lb (454 g) mushrooms, sliced

2 cloves garlic, minced

8–10 red potatoes, cut into small, bite-sized pieces

3 cups (672 g) cooked, shredded chicken

3 cups (681–907 ml) chicken or vegetable broth

1 cup (236 ml) half & half

3 ears of fresh corn, kernels removed and cobs discarded

2 tbsp (30 ml) adobo sauce from a can of chipotle peppers

3 tbsp (28 g) cornstarch mixed with a few tablespoons of cold water (a slurry)

Coarse salt & freshly ground black pepper

BISCUITS
1 can refrigerated biscuits (about 8 large biscuits)

3 tbsp (42 g) butter, melted

2 tsp freshly ground black pepper

1. Press "Saute" to preheat your Instant Pot and set to "Normal." When the word "hot" appears on the display, add the oil, then add the onions, peppers and mushrooms. Cook, stirring occasionally, until the mushrooms release their liquid and it has evaporated, about 7 to 8 minutes. Add the garlic and cook about 1 minute, stirring frequently. Press "Cancel" to turn off the Instant Pot.

2. Add the potatoes, chicken and broth to the pot. Close and lock the lid of the Instant Pot. Press "Manual" and adjust the timer to 15 minutes. Check that the cooking pressure is on "high" and that the release valve is set to "Sealing."

3. When the time is up, open the Instant Pot using "Quick Pressure Release," then switch to the "Saute" setting. Add the half & half, corn and adobo sauce to the pot. Bring the mixture to a boil and add the cornstarch "slurry." Don't add the cornstarch without first mixing it with cold water or it will be a clumpy mess. Stir constantly for about a minute or so to allow the sauce to thicken. Season generously with salt and pepper.

4. To make the biscuits, place the biscuits on a large sheet pan with at least an inch (2.5 cm) between each biscuit. Baste the biscuits liberally with melted butter, then sprinkle the tops with freshly ground black pepper. Bake them according to the directions on the package. Top each bowl of pot pie filling with a biscuit.

My love for Hatch chiles runs deep. I was able to travel to New Mexico a couple of years ago, and I fell in love with its people and culture. I toured Hatch chile farms and ate at restaurants where the chiles they use in their dishes were grown just a few miles away. Whenever I enjoy a dish with authentic Hatch chiles, I swear I can taste the love those beautiful people put into their hard work. This easy pasta dish has all of those flavors and works well for an evening when you want something fast and delicious.

Creamy Hatch Chile Penne

COOK TIME
(UNDER PRESSURE)
6 minutes

YIELD
6 to 8 servings

2 tsp (10 ml) extra-virgin olive oil

1 medium onion, chopped

2 cloves garlic, minced

1 red bell pepper, chopped

1 lb (454 g) dried penne pasta

4 cups (946 ml) chicken broth

½ cup (118 g) chopped Hatch chiles or canned green chiles

1 (15-oz [432-g]) can corn, drained (or the equivalent of fresh corn kernels)

3 cups (500 g) cooked, shredded chicken

½ cup (118 ml) heavy cream

2 cups (226 g) shredded Mexican-blend cheese (or more; see note)

1 tsp coarse salt, or to taste

1 tsp freshly ground black pepper, or to taste

1. Press "Saute" to preheat your Instant Pot. When the word "hot" appears on the display, add the olive oil, then the onions. Cook, stirring occasionally, until the onions are soft, about 5 minutes. Add the garlic and cook about another minute, stirring frequently. Press "Cancel" to turn off the Instant Pot.

2. Add the bell pepper to the pot, then add the pasta and pour the chicken broth over, taking care that all the pasta is submerged. Close and lock the lid of the Instant Pot. Press "Manual" and adjust the timer to 6 minutes. If you're using a different pasta, set the timer for half the time on the package cooking directions. Check that the cooking pressure is on "high" and that the release valve is set to "Sealing."

3. When the time is up, open the Instant Pot using "Quick Pressure Release." Stir the pasta, then add the chiles, corn, chicken, cream and cheese. Stir until it's completely incorporated and the cheese has melted and coated the pasta.

4. Season well with salt and pepper.

NOTE
If desired, you can transfer to a baking dish, top with more cheese and broil a few minutes until the cheese has browned.

These tacos are a combination of two of my favorite flavors: citrus and chipotle. They're reminiscent of tacos al pastor but with a smoky bite. The meat comes out so tender and flavorful, plus it makes great leftovers. Try mixing any leftovers with scrambled eggs in the morning for a quick breakfast.

Chipotle-Citrus Pork Tacos

COOK TIME
(UNDER PRESSURE)
50 minutes

YIELD
8 to 10 servings

2 tsp (10 ml) extra-virgin olive oil

3 lb (1.4 kg) pork shoulder, cut into 4 pieces

½ cup (118 ml) orange juice

1 tbsp (15 ml) white vinegar

¼ cup (32 g) ancho chile powder

2 cloves garlic, minced

1 tsp dried oregano

1 tsp dried cumin

2 canned chipotle peppers, chopped

8 pineapple slices, coarsely chopped (grilled is preferred, see note)

FOR SERVING

Corn tortillas

Chopped white onion

Sliced jalapeño

Chopped cilantro

Sliced avocado

Lime wedges

1. Press "Saute" to preheat your Instant Pot. When the word "hot" appears on the display, add the oil, then brown the pork shoulder in batches on all sides, about 3 to 4 minutes per side. Remove the pork and pour in the orange juice and vinegar, deglaze the pot and scrape up all the brown bits on the bottom.

2. Add the ancho chile powder, garlic, oregano, cumin and chipotle peppers to the pot. Mix well. Place the pork back in the pot, then close and lock the lid. Press "Manual" and adjust the timer to 50 minutes. Check that the cooking pressure is on "high" and that the release valve is set to "Sealing."

3. When the time is up, allow the Instant Pot to naturally release the pressure for 10 minutes, then manually release any remaining pressure. Carefully open the lid and remove the pork to a cutting board. Shred the pork with two forks, then place it in a serving bowl. Drizzle over some of the liquid left in the pot and discard the rest. It's delicious so be generous.

4. Assemble your tacos by putting some pork and onion, sliced jalapeño and chopped cilantro in a corn tortilla. Top with some pineapple, avocado and a squeeze of fresh lime juice.

NOTE
For added flavor, I suggest grilling your pineapple and tortillas on a grill or grill pan. It's not mandatory, but it will make your tacos taste even better!

Whenever chicken breasts are on sale, I like to stock up and make several batches of this Cilantro-Lime Chicken and freeze it, especially since it's so quick and easy to make it in my Instant Pot. You'll love the flavor and you can use it for any number of recipes that call for shredded chicken. We even enjoy it as is, over rice with a side of refried beans.

Cilantro-Lime Chicken Tacos with Charred Jalapeños

COOK TIME
(UNDER PRESSURE)
6 minutes

YIELD
6 to 8 servings

3 tsp (15 ml) extra-virgin olive oil, divided

2 lb (0.9 kg) chicken breast, sliced crosswise into 1-inch (2.5-cm) strips

Juice of 3 limes

3 cloves garlic, minced

½ tsp cumin

½ tsp onion powder

½ tsp chipotle powder

½ tsp coarse salt

½ tsp freshly ground pepper

1 medium chipotle pepper, chopped (from a can of chipotle peppers)

4 jalapeños

FOR SERVING

Flour tortillas

Salsa

Avocado

Chopped cilantro

1. Press "Saute" to preheat your Instant Pot. When the word "hot" appears on the display, add 2 teaspoons (10 ml) of olive oil. Lightly brown the chicken, in batches if necessary, about 3 to 4 minutes. Press "Cancel" to turn off the Instant Pot.

2. Add the lime juice, garlic, cumin, onion powder, chipotle powder, salt, pepper and chipotle pepper to the pot and gently stir to coat the chicken. Close and lock the lid of the Instant Pot. Press "Manual" and adjust the timer to 6 minutes. Check that the cooking pressure is on "high" and that the release valve is set to "Sealing."

3. Meanwhile, place the jalapeños on a sheet pan and toss them with the remaining olive oil. Broil them until lightly charred and blackened, about 5 to 7 minutes. Allow them to cool then slice them crosswise. Set aside.

4. When the time is up, open the Instant Pot using "Quick Pressure Release." Shred the chicken using two forks. Assemble the tacos by putting some chicken onto the flour tortillas and top with the salsa, avocado, jalapeños and cilantro.

This is one of those simple soups that uses a lot of canned ingredients but doesn't taste like it. It's perfect for busy weeknights when I just want something everyone loves and that will only take me a few minutes to prep. This easy soup freezes well, too.

Creamy Taco Soup

COOK TIME
(UNDER PRESSURE)
15 minutes

YIELD
6 to 8 servings

1 tsp extra-virgin olive oil

1 medium onion, chopped

1 lb (454 g) ground beef

1 (1-oz [28-g]) packet taco seasoning

1 (8-oz [226-g]) can tomato sauce

3 (14.5-oz [411-g] each) cans fire-roasted diced tomatoes

1 (4-oz [113-g]) can green chiles

1 (15-oz [425-g]) can corn, drained

1 (15-oz [425-g]) can black beans, drained and rinsed

1 (14.5-oz [411-g]) can chicken broth

4 oz (113 g) cream cheese, cut into 6 pieces

½ cup (118 ml) half & half

Coarse salt and freshly ground black pepper to taste

TOPPINGS
Shredded cheddar cheese

Sour cream

Lime wedges

1. Press "Saute" to preheat your Instant Pot. When the word "hot" appears on the display, add the olive oil, then the onions. Cook about a minute, then add the ground beef. Cook, stirring occasionally, until no pink remains in the beef. Stir in the taco seasoning. Press "Cancel" to turn off the Instant Pot.

2. Add the tomato sauce, tomatoes, green chiles, corn, black beans and chicken broth to the pot and give it a quick stir. Close and lock the lid of the Instant Pot. Press "Manual" and adjust the timer to 15 minutes. Check that the cooking pressure is on "high" and that the release valve is set to "Sealing."

3. When the time is up, open the Instant Pot using "Quick Pressure Release." Add the cream cheese; stir until it's melted and combined. Stir in the half & half, then season well to taste with salt and pepper. Serve with shredded cheese, sour cream and lime wedges.

There's a local Mexican restaurant that has a burrito we all love. It's covered in queso and filled with chicken and chorizo. What's not to love, right? Mexican chorizo has been a favorite of mine for years, but it's greasy and rich. The chicken makes it slightly healthier, yet still keeps the yummy chorizo flavor.

Enchiladas Suizas with Chicken & Mexican Chorizo

COOK TIME
(SLOW COOK)
1 hour

YIELD
4 to 6 servings

1 jalapeño pepper, halved

8 tomatillos, husked, rinsed and halved

2 cloves garlic, peeled

½ white onion, cut into 6 large pieces

1 tbsp (15 ml) olive oil

1 small bunch fresh cilantro, chopped

½ tsp kosher salt, or more to taste

½ tsp freshly ground black pepper, or more to taste

¼ cup (59 ml) vegetable or canola oil

12 corn tortillas

10 oz (280 g) Mexican chorizo, casings removed

2–3 cups (250–375 g) cooked, shredded chicken (use a rotisserie to make your life easy!)

1 cup (236 ml) heavy cream

2 cups (226 g) Mexican-blend shredded cheese, divided

Chopped cilantro, for topping

1. Preheat your broiler to high. On a sheet pan, place the jalapeño pepper cut-side down, the tomatillos cut-side down, and the garlic and white onion. Drizzle with the olive oil. Place under the broiler until the peppers are blackened in spots, about 6 to 8 minutes. Put it all in a high-powered blender along with the cilantro. Blend it until very smooth. Add salt and pepper, to taste.

2. Heat the vegetable oil in a medium skillet over medium-high heat. Fry the corn tortillas, one at a time, until lightly browned and slightly crispy on both sides. Drain on paper towels. Discard the oil.

3. Place the pan back on the stove and reduce the heat to medium. Add the chorizo and cook until it's lightly browned, about 7 to 8 minutes. Stir in the shredded chicken and set aside.

4. Place three tortillas, overlapping as needed, in the bottom of your Instant Pot. Layer with a third of the chorizo-chicken mixture, ½ cup (224 g) shredded cheese, then a third of the tomatillo sauce. Do this twice more, then finish with the last of the tortillas. Pour the cream over the top. Sprinkle on the last ½ cup (113 g) of shredded cheese.

5. Close your Instant Pot and press the "Slow Cooker" setting. Adjust the timer for 1 hour and make sure it's set to "More." When the timer goes off, remove the lid, and sprinkle with cilantro.

Jalapeño poppers are one of my favorite appetizers; more so if they're wrapped in bacon! This easy recipe has all of those flavors baked into a crispy taquito. The Instant Pot takes just 6 minutes cooking time to cook the chicken! You can make and freeze the chicken ahead of time, too, then just thaw and bake.

Jalapeño Popper Taquitos

COOK TIME (UNDER PRESSURE)
6 minutes

YIELD
4 to 6 servings

1 cup (236 ml) chicken broth

2 lb (0.9 kg) boneless, skinless chicken breasts, sliced crosswise into 1-inch (2.5-cm) pieces

Coarse salt and freshly ground black pepper to taste

6 slices bacon, cut crosswise into ½-inch (1.3-cm) pieces

½ cup (118 g) chopped red onion

2 jalapeños, minced

1 clove garlic, minced

1 tsp ancho chile powder

8 oz (226 g) cream cheese, softened

½ cup (56 g) shredded cheddar cheese

10 (6-inch [15-cm]) flour tortillas

1. Pour the chicken broth into your Instant Pot. Season the chicken with salt and pepper, then place it in the pot. Press "Manual" and adjust the timer to 6 minutes. Check that the cooking pressure is on "high" and that the release valve is set to "Sealing."

2. When the time is up, open the Instant Pot using "Quick Pressure Release." Carefully remove the chicken from the pot and place it on a cutting board. Shred the chicken with two forks. Reserve the liquid from the pot and set aside.

3. Press "Saute" to reheat your Instant Pot. When the word "hot" appears on the display, add the bacon and cook until it's browned and crispy, about 8 minutes. Remove the bacon with a slotted spoon and drain it on paper towels. Add the onions and jalapeños to the pot and cook, stirring occasionally, until the onions are soft, about 5 minutes. Add the garlic and ancho chile powder. Cook about another minute, stirring frequently. Add the cream cheese and ½ cup (118 ml) of the reserved liquid to the pot, stirring constantly until it's melted and incorporated. Stir in the shredded cheddar cheese. Remove the pot and set it on a trivet to prevent further cooking.

4. Preheat your oven to 400°F (200°C, or gas mark 6) and grease a large sheet pan with cooking spray. Place about ⅓ cup (80 ml) of the filling in the center of a tortilla, roll it up and place it seam-side down onto the sheet pan. Repeat with the remaining filling and tortillas. Spray the rolled tortillas generously with cooking spray.

5. Bake the taquitos for about 15 minutes, or until tortillas are lightly browned and the filling is hot.

Just like the supporting cast in a movie, a truly great meal needs its side dishes to go from so-so to outstanding. Many Instant Pot owners have invested in a second or even a third pot so they can make an entire meal at once, especially during the summer months to help the house stay cool. I myself own two and am considering a third. You may want to get a steamer basket for the Instant Pot; it makes cooking potatoes and vegetables a breeze.

Simple One-Pot Sides

This simple rice dish has great flavor for so few ingredients. Your Instant Pot makes it so simple, too! Just press "Rice" and it will automatically cook for the perfect amount of time. This rice will go well with any of the recipes from the "Quick and Delicious Mexican Meals" chapter.

Cilantro-Lime Rice

COOK TIME
(RICE SETTING)
Varies

YIELD
4 to 6 servings

2 tbsp (28 g) butter

½ onion, chopped

1 clove garlic, minced

1 cup (185 g) long-grain white rice

1 cup (236 ml) chicken stock

Zest and juice of 1 lime

1 large handful cilantro, chopped

1. Press "Saute" to preheat your Instant Pot and set to "Normal." When the word "hot" appears on the display, add the butter.

2. Once the butter is melted, add the onions and stir to coat. Cook, stirring occasionally, about 5 minutes. Add the garlic and cook about 1 minute, stirring frequently. Press "Cancel" to turn off the Instant Pot.

3. Rinse the rice in a colander and add to the onions in your Instant Pot. NOTE: Do not skip this step. The rice should be wet when added to the Instant Pot as this gives the perfect amount of moisture.

4. Add the chicken stock and stir gently to combine. Place the lid on the Instant Pot then press "Rice" and be sure the release valve is set to "Sealing." No adjustments can be made to time or pressure on the rice setting. When the time is up, wait for the pressure to release naturally. Once all the pressure is released, open your Instant Pot.

5. Add the lime zest, lime juice and cilantro. Stir the rice gently to combine, then fluff the rice with a fork. Serve immediately.

I love caramelized onions so much that I'll serve them as a stand-alone side dish. They're also great mixed into mashed potatoes, as a burger or sandwich topping or even scrambled with eggs. Although this recipe uses the slow-cook setting, you can set the timer to start it whenever you like so it's ready when you are!

Balsamic Caramelized Onions

COOK TIME
(SLOW COOK)
8 hours

YIELD
6 to 8 servings

4 tbsp (56 g) unsalted butter, melted

10 large sweet onions, thickly sliced (about 4–6 slices per onion)

½ cup (118 ml) balsamic vinegar

1 tsp coarse salt, or to taste

1 tsp freshly ground black pepper, or to taste

1. Add the butter and onions to the pot and gently toss to coat the onions. Press "Slow Cook" and set on "less." Cover and cook for 8 hours.

2. Open the Instant Pot and switch to "Saute" mode. Stirring often, allow the liquid created by the onions to simmer and evaporate. Add the balsamic vinegar; stir well. Saute for a few minutes more, stirring frequently, until the balsamic is thick and coats the onions. Season to taste with salt and freshly ground black pepper.

My German heritage meant that we enjoyed a lot of German potato salad when I was a kid. I didn't care for it much then, but now it's one of my absolute favorites. My version uses white balsamic, which my mom and dad both approved—so I think it's a winner. And my Instant Pot takes just 7 minutes to cook the potatoes, which makes this a great weeknight side dish.

German Potato Salad with White Balsamic

COOK TIME
(UNDER PRESSURE)
7 minutes

YIELD
4 to 6 servings

1½ cups (354 ml) water

1½ lb (680 g) russet potatoes, peeled and cut into approximately 8–10 large pieces each

6 slices bacon, cut crosswise into 1-inch (2.5-cm) pieces

1 medium onion, chopped

¼ cup (59 ml) white balsamic vinegar

2 tbsp (24 g) sugar

1 tsp kosher salt

¼ tsp freshly ground black pepper

1 tsp celery seed

2 tbsp (8 g) fresh parsley, chopped

1. Pour the water into the bottom of the pot then place the trivet inside. Carefully layer the potatoes onto the trivet, taking care not to drop any into the water. Close and lock the lid of the Instant Pot. Press "Manual" and adjust the timer to 7 minutes. Check that the cooking pressure is on "high" and that the release valve is set to "Sealing."

2. When the time is up, open the Instant Pot using "Quick Pressure Release." Be careful; there will be a lot of steam and it will be HOT. Carefully remove the potatoes and set them aside.

3. Press "Saute" to reheat your Instant Pot. When the word "hot" appears on the display, add the bacon and cook until it's browned and crispy, about 8 minutes. Remove the bacon with a slotted spoon and drain on paper towels. Add the onions to the bacon drippings. Cook them until they're opaque and softened, about 5 minutes. Stir in the balsamic vinegar, sugar, salt and pepper. Bring it to a boil, then add the potatoes back to the pot, gently stirring them to reheat and help them absorb some of the vinegar mixture. Add the celery seed and fresh parsley. Gently toss to combine. Crumble the bacon and sprinkle on top.

These creamy potatoes are one of my favorite comfort foods. Before my Instant Pot, they were reserved for the holidays. Now I make them at least once a month! They're even delicious cold out of the fridge the next day.

Blue Cheese Potato Gratin

COOK TIME
(UNDER PRESSURE)
6 minutes

YIELD
6 to 8 servings

1 cup (236 ml) chicken broth

3 lb (1.4 kg) russet potatoes, peeled and sliced ¼-inch (0.6-cm) thick

¾ cup (177 ml) heavy cream

1 cup (150 g) crumbled blue cheese

1 tsp kosher salt

½ tsp freshly ground black pepper

½ cup (90 g) grated Parmesan cheese

1. Pour the chicken broth into the Instant Pot. Add the potatoes directly into the pot, taking care to layer them evenly.

2. Close and lock the lid of the Instant Pot. Press "Manual" and adjust the timer to 6 minutes. Check that the cooking pressure is on "high" and that the release valve is set to "Sealing."

3. When the time is up, open the Instant Pot using "Quick Pressure Release." Remove the potatoes with a slotted spoon and place them in a greased 13 x 9-inch (33 x 23-cm) baking dish, leaving the broth in pot. Press "Saute," then add the cream, blue cheese, salt and pepper to the pot. Stir until steaming hot and just starting to bubble and the cheese is completely melted.

4. Pour the sauce over the potatoes, then top the sauce with the Parmesan cheese.

5. Preheat your broiler. Broil the potatoes for 5 to 7 minutes, until the Parmesan is golden brown and the sauce is bubbly hot.

I love corn on the cob topped with just about anything, even just a slather of butter and a little salt. This Whipped Honey Butter is a treat, however, and it really brings out the sweetness of the corn. Serve any extra butter on toast in the morning or with warm corn bread. This recipe goes well with the Beef & Poblano Chili (page 46).

Corn on the Cob with Whipped Honey Butter

COOK TIME
(UNDER PRESSURE)
2 minutes

YIELD
4 servings

1 cup (236 ml) water

4 ears corn, husked

½ cup (114 g) unsalted butter, softened

2 tbsp (42 g) honey

Pinch of salt

Freshly ground black pepper (optional)

1. Pour the water into the pot, then place the trivet inside. Set the corn on top of the trivet.

2. Close and lock the lid of the Instant Pot. Press "Manual" and adjust the timer to 2 minutes. Check that the cooking pressure is on "high" and that the release valve is set to "Sealing."

3. Meanwhile, whip the butter, honey, salt and pepper (if using) in a small mixing bowl. Set aside.

4. When the time is up, open the Instant Pot using "Quick Pressure Release." Remove the corn from the pot and serve it with Whipped Honey Butter.

These mashed potatoes in my Instant Pot are one of my favorite recipes. They come together so quickly, and the Instant Pot keeps them warm for hours if needed. They also get mashed right in the pot—no peeling or draining! They're great made on holidays to keep your oven free, too.

Creamy Mashed Potatoes

COOK TIME
(UNDER PRESSURE)
8 minutes

YIELD
6 to 8 servings

1 cup (236 ml) chicken broth

3 lb (1.4 kg) red potatoes, quartered

4 oz (113 g) cream cheese, softened

½ cup (114 g) butter, very soft

½ cup (118 ml) half & half or heavy cream, room temperature

1. Pour the chicken broth into the pot, then place the trivet inside. Carefully place the potatoes on the trivet. It's fine if a few fall through.

2. Close and lock the lid of the Instant Pot. Press "Manual" and adjust the timer to 8 minutes. Check that the cooking pressure is on "high" and that the release valve is set to "Sealing."

3. When the time is up, open the Instant Pot using "Quick Pressure Release." Remove the trivet from the pot, leaving behind the potatoes and broth. Add the cream cheese, butter and half & half. Mash with a potato masher until smooth. Keep the potatoes on the "warm" setting until ready to serve.

This is a wonderful side dish that we have at least a couple of times a week during the summer months. I've even been known to make it just for myself for dinner plus lunch the next day! Fresh corn in the Instant Pot is so quick and easy, you'll be making it all the time.

Fresh Corn with Tomatoes and Feta

COOK TIME
(UNDER PRESSURE)
2 minutes

YIELD
4 servings

1 cup (236 ml) water

4 ears corn, husked

1 cup (180 g) cherry tomatoes, halved

¼ cup (38 g) feta cheese

¼ cup (10 g) chopped fresh basil leaves

½ tsp coarse salt

½ tsp freshly ground black pepper

1. Pour the water into the pot, then place the trivet inside. Set the corn on top of the trivet.

2. Close and lock the lid of the Instant Pot. Press "Manual" and adjust the timer to 2 minutes. Check that the cooking pressure is on "high" and that the release valve is set to "Sealing."

3. When the time is up, open the Instant Pot using "Quick Pressure Release." Set the corn aside to cool slightly, then remove the kernels from the cobs.

4. In a medium bowl, mix together the corn, tomatoes, feta cheese and fresh basil. Season well with salt and pepper.

These little potatoes are a perfect side dish for dinner, and they're also great with eggs for breakfast. Or toss them in your favorite potato salad recipe for a garlicky twist! Make sure you use the smallest potatoes you can find, or be sure to cut them very small. The cooking time for these potatoes is just 6 minutes, so keep some baby potatoes on hand for a quick, weeknight side dish any day. They go perfectly with the ribs or pork chops from the "Meat Lover's Mains" chapter!

Garlic Baby Potatoes

COOK TIME
(UNDER PRESSURE)
6 minutes

YIELD
4 servings

¼ cup (57 g) butter

4 cloves garlic, minced

1 lb (454 g) tiny baby potatoes, about 1-inch (2.5-cm) thick

½ cup (118 ml) chicken broth

½ tsp coarse salt

½ tsp freshly ground black pepper

1. Press "Saute" to preheat your Instant Pot. When the word "hot" appears on the display, melt the butter, then add the garlic. Cook for 1 minute, stirring frequently. Add the potatoes and toss to coat with the garlic butter.

2. Pour the chicken broth over the potatoes. Close and lock the lid of the Instant Pot. Press "Manual" and adjust the timer to 6 minutes. Check that the cooking pressure is on "high" and that the release valve is set to "Sealing."

3. When the time is up, open the Instant Pot using "Quick Pressure Release." Transfer the potatoes to a serving dish. Season well and serve immediately.

I can't stress enough the importance of using fresh green beans in this recipe. They turn out perfectly crisp-tender with bright flavor from the lemon juice. It's worth the small trouble of trimming fresh beans, I promise! It takes no cooking time at all to make these easy green beans, simply bring the Instant Pot to pressure then immediately release it! You'll love that there's only one pot to clean, no draining blanched beans or sautéing in a separate skillet.

Garlic Butter Green Beans

COOK TIME
(UNDER PRESSURE)
0 minutes
(see note in directions)

YIELD
4 to 6 servings

1 cup (236 ml) water

1 lb (454 g) fresh green beans, cleaned and trimmed

¼ cup (57 g) butter

3 cloves garlic, minced

1 lemon (use the zest of the whole lemon and the juice from half)

½ tsp coarse salt

Freshly ground black pepper to taste

1. Pour the water into the bottom of your Instant Pot. Place the green beans in a steamer basket, then place the basket into the pot. Close and lock the lid of the Instant Pot. Press "Manual" and adjust the timer to 0 minutes. NOTE: This is not a typo; you only need to bring the pot to pressure then release it. Check that the cooking pressure is on "high" and that the release valve is set to "Sealing."

2. When the time is up, open the Instant Pot using "Quick Pressure Release." Carefully remove the beans and set them aside. Pour the water out of the pot and wipe it dry.

3. Put the pot back into the base. Press "Saute" to reheat your Instant Pot. When the word "hot" appears on the display, melt the butter then add the garlic and cook for 1 minute. Press "Cancel" to turn off the Instant Pot. Add the beans back to the pot, then add lemon zest and juice, salt and pepper. Gently stir to coat the beans, then serve.

I'm a serious lover of the combination of lemon and pepper. It's perfect mixed with quinoa for a light, bright side dish. It's such an easy side dish in your Instant Pot because it's just 2 minutes cooking time, too!

Lemon Pepper Quinoa

COOK TIME
(UNDER PRESSURE)
2 minutes

YIELD
6 to 8 servings

1½ cups (255 g) quinoa

1½ cups (354 ml) water

Juice of 1 lemon

1 tsp coarse salt, or to taste

1 tsp freshly ground black pepper, or to taste

1. Press "Saute" to preheat your Instant Pot. When the word "hot" appears on the display, toast the quinoa in your dry pot, stirring frequently, about 5 minutes. Press "Cancel" to turn off the Instant Pot.

2. Add the water to the pot and stir. Close and lock the lid of the Instant Pot. Press "Manual" and adjust the timer to 2 minutes. Check that the cooking pressure is on "high" and that the release valve is set to "Sealing."

3. When the time is up, allow the pressure to release naturally. Do not do a quick release or the quinoa won't be cooked through. Gently stir in the lemon juice, salt and pepper. Serve immediately.

The Instant Pot makes this the quickest side dish you'll ever make. These carrots are sweet, flavorful and perfect for a busy weeknight side dish. Try mashing the carrots and mixing it all together for a fun twist!

Two-Minute Maple-Glazed Carrots

COOK TIME (UNDER PRESSURE)
2 minutes

YIELD
4 to 6 servings

1 cup (236 ml) water

1 lb (454 g) baby carrots

¼ cup (59 ml) maple syrup

2 tbsp (28 g) butter, melted

½ tsp coarse salt

1. Pour the water into the bottom of your Instant Pot, then add the carrots. Close and lock the lid.

2. Press "Manual" and immediately adjust the timer to 2 minutes. Check that the cooking pressure is on "high" and that the release valve is set to "Sealing."

3. When the time is up, open the Instant Pot using "Quick Pressure Release." Drain the carrots with a strainer and place them in a bowl.

4. Meanwhile, mix together the maple syrup, butter and salt. Pour the glaze over the carrots, and toss them gently to coat.

Although these sweet potatoes always remind me of the holidays, we love them enough to make them year-round, especially during the colder months. The Instant Pot makes it so easy and fast! If you like to purchase pre-cut sweet potatoes, you can easily use a steamer basket so they don't fall through.

Maple-Syrup Mashed Sweet Potatoes

COOK TIME
(UNDER PRESSURE)
15 minutes

YIELD
6 to 8 servings

1 cup (236 ml) water

3 lb (1.4 kg) sweet potatoes, peeled and cut into 1-inch (2.5-cm) slices

½ cup (118 ml) whole milk, room temperature

¼ cup (36 g) light brown sugar, loosely packed

⅓ cup (80 ml) maple syrup

½ cup (114 g) butter, softened

½ tsp coarse salt, or to taste

½ tsp freshly ground black pepper, or to taste

1. Pour the water into the bottom of the pot, then place the trivet inside. Carefully layer the potatoes onto the trivet, taking care not to drop any into the water. Start with the larger, flat slices to make your base, then just pile the rest on the top. Close and lock the lid of the Instant Pot. Press "Manual" and adjust the timer to 15 minutes. Check that the cooking pressure is on "high" and that the release valve is set to "Sealing."

2. When the time is up, open the Instant Pot using "Quick Pressure Release." Be careful; there will be a lot of steam and it will be HOT. Carefully pour the potatoes into a colander to strain and discard the water. Put the potatoes back into the Instant Pot.

3. Add the milk, sugar, syrup and butter to the potatoes. Mash with a potato masher until smooth. Season well with salt and pepper.

If you've never tried mashed cauliflower, you're in for a treat! This is my favorite way to serve it, and it couldn't be simpler using your Instant Pot.

Parmesan-Pepper Cauliflower Mash

COOK TIME
(UNDER PRESSURE)
4 minutes

YIELD
4 to 6 servings

2 cups (472 ml) water

1 large head cauliflower, sliced into 10 pieces

2 tbsp (28 g) unsalted butter, softened

¾ cup (135 g) grated Parmesan cheese

1 tsp freshly ground black pepper, or to taste

1 tsp kosher salt, or to taste

1. Pour the water into the Instant Pot, then place a steamer tray inside. Set the cauliflower on top of the steamer tray. Close and lock the lid of the Instant Pot. Press "Manual" and adjust the timer to 4 minutes. Check that the cooking pressure is on "high" and that the release valve is set to "Sealing."

2. When the time is up, open the Instant Pot using "Quick Pressure Release." Carefully lift the steamer tray out of the pot. Be careful; it will be HOT! Place the cauliflower into a large mixing bowl. Reserve ½ cup (118 ml) of the cooking liquid from the pot; discard the rest.

3. Using an immersion blender, puree the cauliflower until very smooth. If the cauliflower is too thick, add a small amount of water until your desired consistency is reached. Stir in the butter, Parmesan cheese and the pepper. Season well to taste with kosher salt.

NOTE
Alternatively, you can use a potato masher in lieu of an immersion blender for a chunkier mash.

Christmas dinner is served at my house every year. I look forward to it, and I used to plan my menu at least a month in advance. These days, I always know that I'll be making prime rib, carrot soufflé and some version of this risotto. Of course, it's so easy and so delicious that it gets made more often than just Christmas, especially now that I make it in my Instant Pot so there's no endless stirring over a hot stove!

Quick Risotto with Wild Mushrooms and Gorgonzola

COOK TIME
(UNDER PRESSURE)
6 minutes

YIELD
6 to 8 servings

1 tbsp (15 ml) extra-virgin olive oil

1 lb (454 g) mushrooms, thickly sliced (I typically use a mix of shitake and crimini)

1 large onion, chopped

2 cloves garlic, minced

1½ cups (296 g) arborio rice

½ cup (118 ml) dry white wine

20 oz (590 ml) low-sodium chicken stock, room temperature

¼ cup (59 ml) heavy cream, room temperature

2 tbsp (19 g) crumbled Gorgonzola cheese

Coarse salt and plenty of freshly ground black pepper, to taste

1. Press "Saute" to preheat your Instant Pot. When the word "hot" appears on the display, add the olive oil, then the mushrooms. Cook the mushrooms, stirring occasionally, until the mushrooms have released their liquid and most of it has evaporated, about 7 to 8 minutes. Add the onions and cook until they're opaque and softened, about 5 minutes. Add the garlic and rice. Cook about another 3 minutes, stirring frequently. Pour in the white wine to deglaze the pot and allow most of it to absorb into the rice. Press "Cancel" to turn off the Instant Pot.

2. Pour the chicken stock into the Instant Pot, and close and lock the lid. Press "Manual" and adjust the timer to 6 minutes. Check that the cooking pressure is on "high" and that the release valve is set to "Sealing."

3. When the time is up, open the Instant Pot using "Quick Pressure Release." Stir in the cream and Gorgonzola. Taste and add more cheese if a stronger flavor is preferred; this will depend on the cheese and your tastes. Season to taste with salt and pepper. If you like pepper, go a little heavy here; it works well in this dish.

I couldn't believe how smooth and creamy these beans were the first time I made them. I've been making Mexican meals for my family for years, but refried beans weren't something I made often because they're so time consuming. Not so with my Instant Pot! Forget soaking your beans in advance and cooking them for hours. These easy refried beans rival any I've made the traditional way. The Instant Pot takes just 50 minutes versus the hours of soaking and cooking time it used to take to make these beans!

Easy Refried Beans

COOK TIME
(UNDER PRESSURE)
50 minutes

YIELD
6 to 8 servings

1 tbsp (15 ml) extra-virgin olive oil

1 medium white onion, chopped

3 cloves garlic, minced

1 tsp dried oregano

1 jalapeño, seeded and minced

1 lb (454 g) dried pinto beans, thoroughly washed and picked over

4 cups (944 ml) chicken broth

4 cups (944 ml) water

1 tsp salt, or to taste

½ cup (56 g) shredded cheddar or Mexican-blend cheese (optional)

1. Press "Saute" to preheat your Instant Pot and set to "Normal." When the word "hot" appears on the display, add the oil to the pot. Add the onions and cook, stirring occasionally, about 5 minutes. Add the garlic, oregano and jalapeño and cook about 1 minute, stirring frequently. Press "Cancel" to turn off the Instant Pot.

2. Add the pinto beans, chicken broth and water to the Instant Pot. Press "Manual" and set timer for 50 minutes, making sure that Instant Pot is set to "high" and that the release valve is set to "Sealing."

3. When the time is up, wait for the pressure to release naturally. Once all the pressure is released, open your Instant Pot. Drain the liquid from the beans, reserving the liquid. I use a colander placed over a large stockpot. Return the beans to the pot, then add some liquid back to the beans. Three-quarters of a cup (177 ml) of liquid gives me the consistency I like, but you can start with ½ cup (118 ml) and add more if you prefer. Using an immersion blender, puree the beans until they're nice and smooth.

4. If you are using the cheese, top the beans with the cheese and put the lid back on. Wait about 5 minutes for the cheese to melt before serving.

Desserts are one of my favorite things to make in my Instant Pot. Recipes that would previously have too many steps—endlessly stirring a rice pudding or having to make a water bath for a cheesecake—are a breeze with my Instant Pot. Many require an oven-safe pan so consider investing in one if you don't already have one on hand. The Coconut Rice Pudding with Fresh Mango is my #1 favorite recipe in this cookbook, so don't miss it!

Easy Weeknight Sweet Treats

I have been making some version of chocolate "pudding" all my life. This is my nod to both my childhood (that's the milk chocolate) and my "adult" life now (that's the semi-sweet). And yes, I quoted "adult" since I like to use that word very loosely! I hope both the kid and the adult in you enjoy this luscious dessert.

Chocolate Pots de Crème

COOK TIME
(UNDER PRESSURE)
6 minutes

YIELD
6 servings

½ cup (118 ml) whole milk

1½ cups (354 ml) heavy cream

3 tbsp (36 g) sugar

6 large egg yolks

¾ cup (135 g) milk chocolate chips

¾ cup (135 g) semi-sweet chocolate chips

Pinch of salt

1 cup (236 ml) water

Whipped cream, for topping

1. Press "Saute" and add the milk, cream and sugar to the pot. Heat until it's very hot and steaming but don't allow it to boil, stirring until the sugar dissolves. Press "Cancel" to turn off the Instant Pot and remove the pot so the cream mixture doesn't scorch.

2. Gently beat the yolks in a medium-sized mixing bowl, then very slowly drizzle in the hot sugar mixture, whisking constantly so the eggs don't cook. Add the chocolate chips and salt. Stir until melted and smooth. Pour the mixture into 6 individual ramekins.

3. Rinse out your pot and wipe it dry. Add the water to the pot, then set your trivet inside. Set 3 ramekins on the trivet, then place a second trivet on top—you can do this step in two cycles if you don't have two trivets. Place the remaining 3 ramekins on the second trivet.

4. Close and lock the lid of the Instant Pot. Press "Manual" and adjust the timer to 6 minutes. Check that the cooking pressure is on "high" and that the release valve is set to "Sealing."

5. When the time is up, allow the pot to release the pressure naturally. Carefully open the lid and remove the ramekins. Cool completely, then refrigerate for a few hours or until fully chilled. Top with freshly whipped cream.

I first began making cheesecake in my Instant Pot in the summertime when I realized I wouldn't have to turn on my oven. Now I use it because I don't have to mess with a water bath or cracks in my cheesecake. This chocolate version is incredibly rich and pairs wonderfully with the fresh, sweet raspberries.

Chocolate Cheesecake with Fresh Raspberries

COOK TIME (UNDER PRESSURE)
40 minutes

YIELD
6 to 8 servings

1 cup (227 g) crushed chocolate sandwich cookies with cream filling (such as Oreos)

2 tbsp (28 g) butter, melted

16 oz (454 g) cream cheese, softened

¾ cup (144 g) sugar

¼ cup (56 g) sour cream

3 large eggs

1 tsp vanilla extract

Pinch salt

1¼ cups (225 g) semi-sweet chocolate chips

1 cup (236 ml) water

2 pints (572 g) fresh raspberries

1. Spray a 7-inch (18-cm) cheesecake pan with a removable bottom with cooking spray. Mix the crushed cookies and butter together, then press them into the bottom of the pan.

2. Beat the cream cheese and sugar in a medium-sized mixing bowl until smooth. Add the sour cream and eggs, one at a time, until fully incorporated. Stir in the vanilla and salt.

3. Melt the chocolate chips by microwaving in 30-second increments until they're melted enough to stir. They should still hold their shape somewhat when you begin stirring. Continue to stir until smooth and all the chips are completely melted. Stir the melted chips into the cheesecake batter.

4. Pour the batter into the cheesecake pan then cover it tightly with foil. Make a foil sling, folding lengthwise twice, then set the cheesecake pan in the center. Pour the water into the pot then put the trivet on top. Place the cheesecake on the sling in the pot, taking care to fold the sling handles down so they don't interfere with closing the pot.

5. Close and lock the lid. Press "Manual" and adjust the timer to 40 minutes. Check that the cooking pressure is on "high" and that the release valve is set to "Sealing."

6. When the time is up, allow the pressure to release naturally for 10 minutes then release any remaining pressure using "Quick Pressure Release." Carefully remove the cheesecake using the sling, then cool it completely on a wire rack. Chill for at least 4 hours. Starting in the center and moving in a circle, top the cheesecake with fresh raspberries.

One of my all-time favorite desserts is sticky rice with sweet mango at our local Thai restaurant. I love that I can create these flavors at home with my Instant Pot with so little effort! Be sure to use arborio rice (the rice used for making risotto), as this will ensure a creamier pudding. Although I prefer using the slow-cook setting for this pudding, I've included instructions for pressure cooking it, too, for those times you just don't want to wait for something sweet!

Coconut Rice Pudding with Fresh Mango

COOK TIME
(SLOW COOK)
2 hours

YIELD
6 to 8 servings

1¼ cups (247 g) arborio rice

3 cups (708 ml) whole milk

1 (14.5-oz [411-g]) can unsweetened coconut milk

½ cup (96 g) sugar

Large pinch of salt

1 tsp vanilla extract

2 cups (330 g) fresh mango chunks

1. Rinse the rice in a fine-mesh strainer under cold water, then place it in your Instant Pot. Add the whole milk, coconut milk, sugar and salt; stir well. Place the lid on top, press "Slow Cook" on your Instant Pot and set to "More." Cook for 2 hours, stirring once halfway through.

2. Open your Instant Pot and stir the pudding. Mix in the vanilla. Pour into individual bowls and top with the fresh mango.

NOTE
If you prefer a thicker pudding, once the slow cooking has completed, switch to "Saute" and cook for several minutes, stirring constantly, until pudding has thickened. Keep in mind that the pudding will thicken as it cools.

PRESSURE COOK METHOD
Close and lock the lid of the Instant Pot. Press "Manual" and adjust the timer to 5 minutes. Check that the cooking pressure is on "high" and that the release valve is set to "Sealing." When the time is up, allow your Instant Pot to release pressure naturally for 10 minutes, then open the Instant Pot using "Quick Pressure Release."

Fresh raspberries go perfectly with Nutella, and when you have bread that's stale, this dessert will become your go-to. I like to time it so that it finishes cooking right about the time we're done with dinner, but if you have guests over and dinner runs long, your Instant Pot will keep this warm for you until you're ready! Add a dollop of whipped cream, a fresh mint leaf or two and a few extra fresh raspberries on top if serving to guests. It makes a nice presentation, especially if you serve it in individual dessert dishes.

Nutella and Raspberry Bread Pudding

COOK TIME
(SLOW COOK)
3 hours

YIELD
6 to 8 servings

½ cup (148 g) Nutella or other chocolate-hazelnut spread

8 slices artisan french bread, preferably stale (or dry it out in a 200°F [93°C] oven for about 10 minutes if it's fresh)

2 large eggs

½ cup (96 g) sugar

1¼ cups (295 ml) half & half

1 tsp vanilla extract

¼ tsp salt

1 pint (286 g) fresh raspberries (reserve a few for garnish)

Whipped cream, ice cream or chocolate sauce, for topping

1. Spread the Nutella onto four slices of bread, dividing it equally. Place the remaining bread slices on top, then cut up the "sandwiches" into bite-sized pieces. Set aside.

2. Place the eggs and sugar in your Instant Pot and whisk thoroughly. Add the half & half, vanilla and salt, then whisk to combine.

3. Spray the pot with cooking spray. Add the bread cubes, stirring gently to combine, pressing down to ensure it's all submerged. Cover and refrigerate for at least an hour. Add the raspberries and mix well.

4. Place in the Instant Pot and close the lid. Press "Slow Cook" and set to "less," then adjust the timer for 3 hours.

5. Serve with whipped cream, ice cream or a drizzle of chocolate sauce . . . or all three! Garnish with a few fresh raspberries.

Making applesauce is the easiest thing in the world with your Instant Pot! My daughter Katie requests this all the time, and it's rare that we don't have a batch in our fridge. The best part is there's no need to peel your apples! Just don't forget to remove the cinnamon stick before pureeing. Yes, I'm talking from experience . . . .

Strawberry Applesauce

COOK TIME
(UNDER PRESSURE)
5 minutes

YIELD
8 to 10 servings

¼ cup (56 ml) water

3 lb (1.4 kg) Gala apples, quartered (stem and core removed; no need to peel)

12 strawberries

¼ cup (48 g) sugar

1 cinnamon stick

Juice of 1 lemon

Pinch of salt

1. Place the water, apples, strawberries, sugar, cinnamon stick, lemon juice and salt into your Instant Pot. Close and lock the lid, press "Manual" and adjust the timer to 5 minutes. Check that the cooking pressure is on "high" and that the release valve is set to "Sealing."

2. When the time is up, allow your Instant Pot to release pressure naturally. Once the pressure is released, open the pot and remove the cinnamon stick. Using an immersion blender, blend your applesauce to your desired consistency.

NOTE
If you don't have an immersion blender, you may also use a regular blender, in batches if necessary.

This easy cheesecake is beloved by everyone in my family. Even people who claim not to care much for cheesecake LOVE this recipe. I originally made it for my mom who loves all things lemon, but I make it often because everyone claims it's a favorite. Your family will love this one, too. It's easy to mix together and the Instant Pot "bakes" it in just 30 minutes!

Lemon Gingersnap Cheesecake

COOK TIME
(UNDER PRESSURE)
30 minutes

YIELD
6 slices

1½ cups (340 g) finely crushed gingersnaps

6 tbsp (84 g) butter, melted

16 oz (454 g) cream cheese, softened

½ cup (96 g) sugar

2 large eggs

Zest from 1 lemon

1 tbsp (15 ml) lemon juice

1 tsp pure vanilla extract

1 cup (236 ml) water

1 pint (286 g) fresh raspberries, for topping

1. Spray a 7-inch (18-cm) cheesecake pan with a removable bottom with cooking spray. Mix the gingersnaps and butter together, then press the mixture firmly into the bottom of the pan.

2. In a medium-sized mixing bowl, beat the cream cheese and sugar until smooth. Add the eggs, one at a time, and mix until they're fully incorporated. Mix in the lemon zest, lemon juice and vanilla.

3. Pour the batter into the cheesecake pan, then cover it with foil. Make a foil sling by folding a sheet of foil lengthwise twice, then set the cheesecake pan in the center. Pour the water into the pot, then place the trivet on the bottom. Place the cheesecake on the sling in the pot, taking care to fold the sling handles down so they don't interfere with closing the pot.

4. Close and lock the lid. Press "Manual" and adjust the timer to 30 minutes. Check that the cooking pressure is on "high" and that the release valve is set to "Sealing."

5. When the time is up, allow the pressure to release naturally for 15 minutes, then release any remaining pressure using "Quick Pressure Release." Carefully remove the cheesecake using the sling, then cool it completely on a wire rack. Gently dab any condensation from the top of the cheesecake before cooling. Chill for at least 4 hours. Top the cheesecake with fresh raspberries.

NOTE
This cheesecake has a fairly thick gingersnap crust. If you prefer, you can reduce the amounts to 1 cup (226 g) of finely crushed gingersnaps and 4 tablespoons (56 g) of melted butter.

Who doesn't love a dessert with just 4 minutes cooking time? These easy peaches are perfect on their own or as an accompaniment to vanilla ice cream. Be sure to use large peaches that are ripe but not soft.

Streusel "Baked" Peaches

COOK TIME
(UNDER PRESSURE)
4 minutes

YIELD
4 servings

⅓ cup (27 g) regular oats

2 tbsp (15 g) flour

¼ cup (36 g) light brown sugar, loosely packed

¼ tsp cinnamon

¼ tsp salt

¼ cup (56 g) cold butter, cut into 12 cubes

¼ cup (57 g) pecans, chopped

2 large peaches, halved

1 cup (236 ml) water

Ice cream or fresh whipped cream, for serving (optional)

1. Mix together the oats, flour, brown sugar, cinnamon and salt in a small mixing bowl. Add the butter. Using a fork or your fingers, "cut" the butter into the oat mixture. Fold in the pecans.

2. Top each peach half with a quarter of the streusel, packing it down as necessary to ensure it sticks.

3. Fill your pot with the water, then top with the trivet. Carefully place the stuffed peaches onto the trivet. Don't be concerned if a tiny bit of the topping falls through. Close and lock the lid of the Instant Pot. Press "Manual" and adjust the timer to 4 minutes. Check that the cooking pressure is on "high" and that the release valve is set to "Sealing."

4. When the time is up, open the Instant Pot using "Quick Pressure Release." Remove the peaches from the pot and serve with ice cream, fresh whipped cream or just as is!

This simple, yet elegant, dessert comes together so quickly in your Instant Pot you won't believe it! It's perfect for a dinner party because the Instant Pot keeps the pears warm until you're ready to serve. Serve them on their own or drizzle with the chocolate sauce for an extra-special treat.

Vanilla Poached Pears with Luscious Chocolate Sauce

COOK TIME
(SLOW COOK)
30 minutes
(UNDER PRESSURE)
3 minutes

YIELD
4 servings

LUSCIOUS CHOCOLATE SAUCE

2 cups (454 g) dark chocolate chunks

1 cup (336 ml) heavy cream

1 tsp vanilla extract

2 tbsp (30 ml) Grand Marnier (optional)

PEARS

5 cups (1.2 L) water

2 cups (454 g) sugar

1 cinnamon stick

1 vanilla bean

4 ripe pears, peeled

1. Make the sauce first. Press "Slow Cook" on your Instant Pot and set to "high." Add the chocolate and cream to the pot. Cover and heat for 30 minutes, stirring once halfway through the cooking time.

2. Open the lid and stir until combined. Stir in the vanilla and Grand Marnier (if using). Set aside and clean out the Instant Pot to make the pears.

3. Press "Saute" to reheat the pot. Pour the water and sugar into the pot. Heat, stirring frequently, until the sugar is dissolved. Add the cinnamon stick and vanilla bean to the pot, then nestle the pears into the liquid.

4. Close and lock the lid of the Instant Pot. Press "Manual" and adjust the timer to 3 minutes. Check that the cooking pressure is on "high" and that the release valve is set to "Sealing."

5. When the time is up, open the Instant Pot using "Quick Pressure Release." Remove the pears from the pot and serve them with a generous amount of the Luscious Chocolate Sauce.

NOTE
You can also make this chocolate sauce on the stove over low heat. The slow-cook method allows you to keep it warm indefinitely. If serving immediately, the stove-top method is a good alternative.

Acknowledgments

I have so many people to thank for helping me while I wrote this book and for getting me to this beautiful place in life where I was able to do so. Sincerest thanks to the following people:

Mom and Dad, for washing all those dishes! And, of course, for the unwavering support, love and inspiration you've given me since the day I was born. I love you.

My daughter Kylie, for your brilliant sense of self and style.
My daughter Katie, for your kind soul and an endless smile that lights up the world.
And to you both for making me laugh and smile every single day. I couldn't be prouder of the kind, smart, beautiful girls you are.

Robert Wadsworth, the best friend a girl could ask for.

My agent, Tim Kessler, for always having my back and for countless laughs over the years!

My hardworking publisher and team, for taking a chance on a first-time author. Special thanks to Sarah Monroe, who held my hand throughout the process and whose feedback and guidance are so appreciated. I couldn't have done it without you.

To the dear friends, bloggers, chefs and foodies who have selflessly offered support, laughter and knowledge over the span of many years. You have each impacted my personal life or career in some way and I am thankful for you.

In no particular order: Maryanne Roy, Lala Montano, Suzanne Spence, Sarah Holly, Scott and Rachael Hoynoski, Keith Whelpley and Rachel Schneider, Curt Walker, Pamela Johnson, Francis Unson, Jill Bonds, Mark Berriman, Kristin Carlson, Shelly Burnett and Jake Peña, Monica Bhide, Lisa Haskins, Jolie Smith, Kelly Heppner, Alan Bernardo, Amy Flanigan, Becca Heflin-Donovan, Tess Masters, Jeffrey Saad, Kimberly Engel, April Gremillion, Pamela McCarthy, Aaron Borrelli, Tom Bruno, Jim and Connie Mommsen, Rob and Britt Aerts, Kurt Calder, Kelly Moyzes, Louise Scauzillo, David White, Andrea Meyers, Amy McBurney, Carrie Dahlgren Larson, Alice D'Antoni Phillips, Wendi Higginbotham (and her Szechuan Beef), Sara Poole, Jeanette Albright, Daniel Anderson, Steve Myers.

My friend, Lisa Wixom, and anyone and everyone who suffers from depression, alcoholism or mental illness: I still miss you every day, Grasshopper.

About the Author

Kristy Bernardo is the creator of the popular food blog The Wicked Noodle, and she has been an influential member of the food blogging world for more than ten years. Although mostly self-taught, she has been strongly influenced by her mother and grandmother and honed her skills at boot camp at the Culinary Institute of America in Hyde Park, NY. She has owned a successful business as a personal chef, has taught cooking classes to all ages, speaks at conferences and events and has appeared regularly on video and television. Her work as both a food and travel writer have appeared in numerous mainstream online publications, such as Huffington Post, *Food & Wine* magazine, *Better Homes and Gardens* and many more.

Kristy lives in northern Virginia with her two daughters, Kylie and Katie, and their two cats, Mr. Pepper and Princess Whiskers. You can most often find her walking or biking the nearby trails, creating in her kitchen or trying new cocktails at restaurants everywhere.

Index